SPAD VII
vs
ALBATROS D III
1917–18

JON GUTTMAN

First published in Great Britain in 2011 by Osprey Publishing,
Midland House, West Way, Botley, Oxford OX2 0PH, UK
443 Park Avenue South, New York, NY 10016, USA
E-mail: info@ospreypublishing.com

A CIP catalogue record for this book is available from the British Library

ISBN: 978 1 84908 475 8
PDF e-book ISBN 978 1 84908 476 5

Edited by Tony Holmes
Cover artwork, cockpit and armament scrap views by Jim Laurier
Three-views by Harry Dempsey
Battlescene by Mark Postlethwaite
Page layout by Ken Vail Graphic Design, Cambridge, UK
Index by Alan Thatcher
Typeset in A Garamond
Maps by bounford.com
Originated by PDQ Digital Media Solutions, Suffolk, UK
Printed in China through Bookbuilders

11 12 13 14 15   10 9 8 7 6 5 4 3 2 1

Cover Art
On 22 April 1917, SPAD VIIs of the Royal Flying Corps' No. 23 Sqn and
Sopwith Pups of the Royal Naval Air Service's 3 Naval Squadron were
escorting FE 2bs of No. 18 Sqn on a bombing mission when the SPADs
became separated from the rest of the formation. At 1900 hrs the No. 23
Sqn pilots spotted what they thought to be British aircraft at higher altitude
between the French town of Marcoing and Havrincourt Wood, but as they
climbed to join them, they suddenly came under attack from what turned
out to be a mixed formation of Albatros D IIIs from *Jastas* 5 and 12. At
2005 hrs two SPADs were brought down south of Marcoing by *Jasta* 12's
CO, Hptm Paul Henning Adalbert Theodor von Osterroht, and *Jasta* 5's
Offstv Edmund Nathanael, whose victim fell at Ribécourt-la-Tour for his
fifth victory. 2Lts K. R. Furniss (A6695) and F. C. Craig (A6682) were
captured, Furniss subsequently dying of his wounds. At 2010 hrs Vzfw
Reinhold Jörke of *Jasta* 12 was credited with a SPAD downed in Allied
lines, its pilot Capt Kenneth C. McCallum, being wounded in action.
Vzfw Ernst Dahlmann claimed a SPAD over *Jasta* 5's old aerodrome at
Gonnelieu, but it was disallowed. *Jasta* 12's Ltn d R Friedrich Roth was also
credited with an aeroplane over Marcoing at 2005 hrs, but No. 23 Sqn
suffered no further casualties. Although the Germans lost no men, No. 23
Sqn claimed three Albatros D IIIs out of control – one east of Cambrai at
1820 hrs by 2Lt R. L. Keller and two over Fontaine Notre Dame at 1830
hrs and Flequières at 1900 hrs by Capt William J. C. Kennedy-Cochran-
Patrick. Coincidentally, both Nathanael's and Kennedy-Cochran-Patrick's
successes brought their respective scores up to five. (Artwork by Jim
Laurier)

Acknowledgements
Thanks to Frank W. Bailey, Norman Franks, Roberto Gentilli, Alan Toelle,
Paolo Varriale and Greg VanWyngarden, as well as the late aces Pierre de
Cazenove de Pradines, Francesco Carlo Lombardi and André Martenot de
Cordoux for their assistance in preparing this volume.

German ranks	French ranks	Italian ranks	RFC ranks
Major	Commandant	Maggiore	Major
Rittmeister (Rittm)	Cavalry Captain	Capitano di Cavalleria	Cavalry Captain
Hauptmann (Hptm)	Capitaine	Capitano	Army Captain
Oberleutnant (Oblt)	Lieutenant	Tenente	Lieutenant
Leutnant (Ltn)	Sous-Lieutenant	Sottotenente	Second Lieutenant
Offizierstellvertreter (Offstv)	Adjutant	-	Warrant Officer
Feldwebel	Sergent-Chef	-	Master Sergeant
Vizefeldwebel (Vzfw)	Maréchal-des-Logis	-	Sergeant First Class
Sergeant	Sergent	Sergente	Sergeant
Unteroffizier (Uffz)	Caporal	Caporale	Corporal
Gefreiter (Gfr)	Brigadier	-	Private First Class
Flieger (Flgr)	Soldat	Soldato	Private

CONTENTS

INTRODUCTION

Although eclipsed in fame by the SPAD XIII that evolved from it, the French SPAD VII occupies a special place in the annals of World War I aviation for the exceptional balance it struck in its time between airframe, engine and armament. When most fighter aircraft entering service in 1916 were improvisations, the SPAD designers managed to combine an innovative engine with the robust airframe of a failed two-seat fighter design and the newly developed synchronised machine gun to produce a remarkably efficient warplane.

So sound was the SPAD VII's basic design that even when more potent progeny were developed, it remained in use, with an adjustable radiator and a more powerful engine, right to the end of the conflict. If, as happened all too often, the spur reduction gear in the faster and more heavily armed SPAD XIII should break down, French fighter pilots would fall back on the VII, with its more reliable direct-drive engine, and still have a reasonable chance against their German opponents.

At one time or another, the SPAD VII served with the air arms of France, Britain, Russia, Belgium, Italy and the United States. SPAD VIIs were also flown with distinction by other volunteers in the French *Aéronautique Militaire*, hailing from distant or belated allies such as Japan and Portugal, and such diverse neutral nations as Argentina, Switzerland and China. The aces who flew them included France's greatest – René Fonck, Georges Guynemer, Georges Madon, Armand Pinsard, René Dorme, Alfred Heurtaux and Albert Deullin – as well as American Raoul Lufbery of the *Escadrille* Lafayette, Italian ace of aces Francesco Baracca, Russian's Ivan Smirnov and third-ranking Belgian ace Edmond Thieffry. Even two German aces, Eduard *Ritter* von Schleich and Rudolf Windisch, reportedly flew captured SPAD VIIs on a few occasions.

The fighter's arrival on the Western Front in August 1916 would have constituted a serious threat to German air superiority there had it not coincided with the debut

of some formidable Teutonic counterparts in the form of the Albatros D I and D II. Sturdy biplanes with sleek plywood fuselages, this deadly duo were not quite as manoeuvrable as the SPAD VII, but they more than made up for this with the much deadlier firepower offered by twin synchronised machine guns. Combined with the tactical doctrine devised by their greatest proponent, Hptm Oswald Boelcke, the Albatros biplanes contained the threat of improved Allied fighters and took a heavy toll on British and French aircraft in general during the last few months of 1916.

SPAD VIIs of *escadrille* SPA15, bearing the red plumed helm of le Chevalier Bayard as a unit insignia, line up for their next mission in the Chemin des Dames sector during the late spring of 1917. (SHAA B77.1832)

At the end of the year Albatros introduced a new offspring of the D II featuring a sesquiplane arrangement that consisted of a two-spar upper wing and single-spar lower plane inspired by France's successful Nieuport 11, 16 and 17 scouts. This machine, the D III, offered the improved downward visibility and manoeuvrability of its Nieuport counterparts, but within a month of its arrival in frontline units the scout displayed a serious weakness. Due to the fact that the aircraft was both heavier and more powerful than the radial-engined Nieuports, the Albatros' lower wings had an even greater tendency than the French scouts to suffer structural failure in high-speed dives or when placed under other stresses.

Withdrawn for almost two months while Albatros reinforced its lower wing structure, the D III returned to the *Jagdstaffeln* (or *Jastas*) in time for concurrent offensives by the French and British in April 1917. Flown by the most experienced German airmen, the D IIIs had their moment of glory in an aerial slaughter that the British came to call 'Bloody April'. It was during this time that Manfred *Freiherr* von Richthofen reached his personal apogee as a fighter pilot, scoring a quarter of his 80 victories in the course of the month and earning immortal notoriety for his all-red

This rare photograph of a SPAD VII from SPA65 in flight shows off the aeroplane's distinctive silhouette. (SHAA B89.1513)

Albatros D III long before he laid eyes on a Fokker triplane. Several others in von Richthofen's *Jasta* 11, including his brother Lothar, also added considerably to their tallies, as did a number of other German aces.

Over the following few months an even sleeker, lightened version of the Albatros D III, the D V, began to take its place on *Jasta* strength – but not entirely, for the lower wing flutter and outright failure that had temporarily set back the D III's introduction recurred to an even more disturbing extent on the D V. While Albatros strove to remedy the problems afflicting its new scout, the D III remained in production both with the parent company and its subsidiary, the Ostdeutsche Albatros Werke (OAW), into the autumn of 1917. Indeed, the steps taken to reinforce the D III's lower wing had been so effective that there were very few reports of structural failures afflicting the OAW-built version.

Even while the twin-gun SPAD XIII and strengthened Albatros D Va were replacing them on the Western Front, the SPAD VII and Albatros D III had a second opportunity to square off over Italy's Isonzo River in the late autumn of 1917. There, imported SPAD VIIs were flown by some of the top *squadriglie* in the Italian army air force, while D IIIs, appearing in three *Jastas* despatched to support a German army contingent in Austria, were joined by licence-built Austrian variants produced by the Oesterreichische Flugzeugfabrik Allgemeine Gesellschaft (Oeffag). These machines would eventually evolve into the best Albatros fighters of the war, and the best fighters in the *Kaiserliche und Königliche Luftfahrtruppen*.

These then were classic adversaries that represented something of a study in contrasts. Dominating the French side and serving smaller but not inconsiderable roles among the British and Italians was the SPAD VII, boasting one of the war's sturdiest airframes but armed with a single machine gun that had a disturbing tendency to jam. Serving for several months as the mainstay of the German fighter arm, the Albatros D III offered superior firepower, but also a wing cellule that represented a developmental dead end that had been retained rather longer than was healthy. Those intrinsic differences aside, as was so often the case during the first air war, individual pilot skill and tactical doctrine tended to be the ultimate arbiter of each duel's outcome.

Albatros D IIIs of *Jasta* 12 warm up at Epinoy aerodrome in the late winter of 1917, shortly before the unit's move to Roucourt on 12 April. The aeroplane at far left was flown by Ltn d R Friedrich Hochstetter, who downed a Sopwith Pup on 26 May. He marked his fighter with three stacked black cannonballs in memory of his prior artillery service. Next in line is the aeroplane of the commander, Hptm Paul Henning von Osterroht. (Greg VanWyngarden)

A SPAD VII bearing the sun insignia of *escadrille* N102 and a personal tail marking sits before a camouflaged Bessonneaux hangar in 1917. (SHAA B83.70)

CHRONOLOGY

1915

27 February   Louis Béchereau of the Société anonyme pour l'Aviation et ses derives (SPAD) applies for a patent for a tractor biplane with a gunner's nacelle suspended by struts in front of the propeller, as well as single-bay wings braced with an intermediate set of articulated auxiliary struts.

May   SPAD SA 1 evaluated, leading to a series of two-seat rotary engine fighters before Béchereau abandons the arrangement.

1916

March   SPAD tests the SH, incorporating a 140hp Hispano-Suiza 8A engine in a single-seat version of its SA airframe.

10 May   *Aéronautique Militaire* places its first order for 248 SPAD single-seat scouts.

June   *Idflieg* orders three prototype Albatros D IIIs (D IIs incorporating sesquiplane wing cellules inspired by the Nieuport 11 and 17).

July   SPAD tests its type V (powered by a 150hp Hispano-Suiza 8Aa), which evolves into the SPAD VII.

Summer   Robert Thelen's Albatros D I and D II fighter designs are tested and accepted for production by the *Inspektion der Fliegertruppen* (*Idflieg*).

August   SPAD VIIs commence frontline service.

16 September   Albatros D Is and D IIs see their first combat with *Jasta* 2, Ltn Otto Walter Höhne bringing down an FE 2b.

17 September   Hptm Oswald Boelcke leads *Jasta* 2 in a demonstration of team effort against BE 2cs and FE 2bs that results in five victories, including the first for Ltn Manfred *Freiherr* von Richthofen.

October   After testing the prototypes in September, *Idflieg* orders 400 Albatros D IIIs.

December   Seeking to improve SPAD performance, Hispano-Suiza develops high-compression 180hp 8Ab and larger 200hp reduction geared 8B engines.

21 December   First three Albatros D IIIs arrive at *Jasta* 24.

1917

17 January   *Armee Oberkommando* 2 reports first four cases of 'Rib fractures and breakage of the leading edge' in Albatros D IIIs during the course of turning manoeuvres and diving.

24 January   Ltn Manfred von Richthofen, now commanding *Jasta* 11, suffers lower wing failure and *Jasta* 'Boelcke' reports three similar incidents, one of which kills five-victory ace Offstv Leopold Reimann, leading to the Albatros D III's withdrawal for structural reinforcement.

February   SPAD XIII, powered by a Hispano-Suiza 8B engine, is ordered into production. The Oesterreichische Flugeugwerke AG (Oeffag) produces its first licence-built Albatros D III, but wing structural concerns delay its delivery pending further testing and additional reinforcement.

March	First SPAD VIIs arrive in Italy.
April	Strengthened Albatros D IIIs return to frontline German service. First SPAD XIIIs arrive on the Western Front for evaluation.
9 April–17 May	Battles of Arras and Vimy Ridge precipitate 'Bloody April' for the RFC.
16-20 April	France's Nivelle Offensive begins, including the Second Battle of the Aisne and the Battle of Chemin des Dames.
21 April	Albatros informs *Idflieg* of its 'lightened Albatros D III airframe' and duly receives a first order for 200 D Vs.
May	First SPAD VIIs enter frontline Italian service with *70ª Squadriglia*.
17 May	Oeffag-built Albatros D III undergoes testing at Fischamend, leading to frontline delivery in June.
13 June	Capt Frederick Sowrey of No. 19 Sqn RFC scores the first SPAD XIII victory.
23 June	In response to the United States' declaration of war on 6 April 1917, Germany launches the *Amerika Programm*, doubling the number of fighter units and necessitating continued Albatros production to equip them.
20 August	Capt Georges Guynemer of *escadrille* N3 uses newly delivered SPAD XIII S504 to shoot down a DFW C V for his 53rd, and last, victory.
September	While reinforced Albatros produces reinforced D Vs and D Vas, *Idflieg* places a final D III order with Ostdeutsche Albatros Werke (OAW).
22 October	Capt Francesco Baracca scores Italy's first SPAD XIII victory, and the nation's first over a German aircraft.
24-26 October	Battle of Caporetto results in a rout of the Italian army, which retreats to Piave River.
December	French units report 131 SPAD XIIIs in frontline service, but engine problems, mostly with the Hispano-Suiza 8B's spur reduction gear, ground them two days out of three. SPAD VIIs remain in service until the end of the war.

Albatros D IIIs of *Jasta* 12 in May 1917 after the death of Hptm Paul Henning von Osterroht on 23 April and his replacement with Oblt Adolf von Tutschek, who used his all-black, white-nosed aeroplane as a model for the black tails and front cowlings and white spinners adopted as the unit motif. The swastika-marked D III in the middle is believed to be that of Ltn Paul Billik. (Greg VanWyngarden)

DESIGN AND DEVELOPMENT

SPAD VII

SPAD SA 2 S.17, complete with tricolour fuselage bands, shows the odd observer's 'pulpit', which proved a failure, and the robust fuselage, wing cellule and tail, all of which proved fundamentally sound enough to allow the aeroplane to be redesigned as a single-seat fighter. (Greg VanWyngarden)

The SPAD VII was a serendipitous mating of an innovative powerplant with a sound airframe. It was also a classic case of concocting a sublime lemonade from a bitter lemon.

The aeroplane's builder was originally called the Societé provisoire des aéroplanes Deperdussin until its dissolution in August 1914, followed by its resurrection as the Société anonyme pour l'Aviation et ses derives. Besides retaining the original company acronym, SPAD also kept Deperdussin's talented designer, Louis Béchereau.

Following France's declaration of war on the Central Powers on 2 August 1914, SPAD's design team produced a small tractor biplane with ailerons on all wing surfaces powered by an 80hp Le Rhône 9C rotary engine. The aircraft featured a machine gunner's nacelle mounted ahead of the airscrew by struts attached to the upper wing and undercarriage. Introduced in late 1915, the SPAD SA 1 and its successors – the 110hp Le Rhône 9J-powered SA 2 and the SA 4, which reverted to the 80hp 9C due to cooling problems, and which featured ailerons on the upper wing only – were more intimidating to the occupant of the front 'pulpit', who stood little chance of survival in the event of a noseover upon

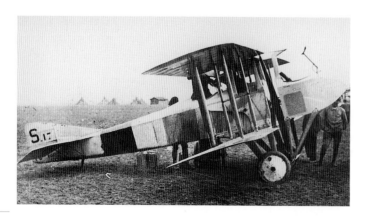

landing, than to the enemy. The last of the SA types were out of French service by May 1916, although as many as 67 remained in Russian use until as late as June 1917.

Although SPAD's two-seat fighter concept was a failure, its basic airframe was promisingly robust. On 4 June 1915 Béchereau applied for a patent for its single-bay wing cellule, which featured an intermediate set of narrow-chord articulated struts, to which the bracing wires were attached at the midpoint. That arrangement added strength and, by reducing vibration in the wires, reduced drag as well.

Béchereau's next fighter, the SPAD SG, was essentially a single-seat SA 4 with a remotely controlled Hotchkiss machine gun in an unmanned front nacelle. Evaluated in April 1916, it too was a failure, but then Béchereau altered the airframe to use a new aluminium-block, 140hp, Hispano-Suiza 8A V8 water-cooled engine developed by Swiss-born engineer Marc Birkigt. By then, too, Béchereau had been able to replace the awkward front gun nacelle with a 0.303-in Vickers machine gun installed directly in front of the pilot, firing through the propeller using cam-activated interrupter gear devised by Birkigt for his own engine.

Originally designated the SPAD SH, the prototype had a large conical spinner in front of a circular radiator and underwent flight-testing in March 1916. The spinner was soon abandoned, but the rounded radiator shell was retained. A further development, using a 150hp Hispano-Suiza 8Aa engine that was designated the SPAD 5, underwent evaluation in July, reportedly reaching a maximum speed of 170 kilometres per hour and climbing to 3,000 metres in nine minutes.

Already impressed with the fighter's fundamental design, the *Aéronautique Militaire* had placed an order for 268 on 10 May 1916. The final production variant was officially designated the SPAD 7.C1 (the 'C1' indicating that it was a single-seat *chasseur*, or fighter), but was more widely known as the SPAD VII.

Allegedly, the first pilot to receive a SPAD VII was Lt Armand Pinsard of N26, who used S122 to force an LVG to land between Combles and Rancourt on 23 August 1916. That was not confirmed, but on 7 September he used S122 to drive an enemy aeroplane down near Pertain, where British artillery demolished it. Pinsard followed that up with a second victory near Lechelle on 1 November. Later in the month he left N26 to take command of N78, and while with this unit Pinsard would claim a further 15 victories. He would survive the war with a final tally of 27.

On 2 September a SPAD VII went to Sgt Paul Sauvage of N65 and others were delivered to the famed *escadrille* N3 'Les Cigognes'. Among the latter, S115 was assigned to Sous-Lt Georges Guynemer, who used it two days later to shoot down an Aviatik C II over Hyencourt for his 15th victory. Ltns Hans Steiner and Otto Fresenius of *Kampfstaffel* 37 were killed.

On 23 September Guynemer downed two Fokkers, plus a third

SPAD VII S154 of N62 sits outside a Bessonneaux hangar in the winter of 1916–17. Incidents of mistaken identity may lie behind the additional French roundels on the tailplane as well as the tricolour fuselage band. (SHAA B76.1141)

11

SPAD VII

19ft 11in.

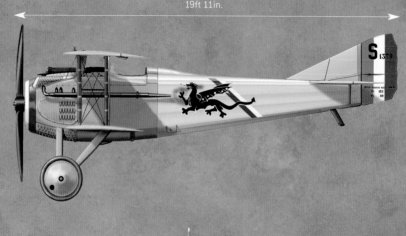

7ft 3in.

25ft 8in.

unconfirmed. As he returned over the lines at an altitude of 3,000 metres, nervous French anti-aircraft gunners struck his unfamiliar looking aeroplane with a 75mm shell, shattering the water reservoir and tearing fabric from the left upper wing. Guynemer spun down, but managed to regain control and pull up at about 180 metres, before crash-landing in a shell hole. Emerging with a cut knee and a slight concussion, Guynemer wrote to his father, 'Only the fuselage was left, but it was intact. The SPAD is solid. With another aeroplane I would now be thinner than this piece of paper'.

Completely sold on the new fighter, Guynemer was back in action soon after receiving S132 on 25 September. On that same day N3's commander, Lt Alfred Heurtaux, scored his third victory since receiving SPAD VII S113 – and his eighth overall – when he destroyed a 'Fokker' over Villers Carbonnel. This turned out in fact to be a Halberstadt D II, and his victim, Ltn Kurt Wintgens of *Jasta* 1, an 18-victory ace and holder of the *Orden Pour le Mérite*.

By the end of the month, 24 SPAD VIIs had reached the front, and N3's aces in particular had quickly adjusted the tactics they had previously employed in the nimble Nieuports to take advantage of their new fighters' durability and speed. The SPAD soon eclipsed the Nieuport as the French *chasseurs'* weapon of choice, and likewise began making its way into the hands of their allies. Britain was swift to see the SPAD VII's worth but relatively slow to get it into frontline service. Three were delivered to No. 60 Sqn, Royal Flying Corps (RFC), for evaluation in September 1916, and on 28 September Capt Ernest L. Foot used S126 – given the British serial number A253 – to attack four Albatros two-seaters over Avesnes les Bapaume, downing one for his fourth victory.

On 30 September the RFC commander, Maj Gen Hugh M. Trenchard, asked for 30 more SPADs and on 5 October the French Ministry of War authorised the purchase of airframes, with the understanding that Britain would supply the engines. That same month the first SPADs arrived to replace No. 19 Sqn's BE 12s, although the unit would not be completely re-equipped until February 1917. February also

OPPOSITE
SPAD VII of Cpl Marcel Henriot, N65, based at Bonne-Maison in April 1917. Born on 3 September 1896 in Saulnat (Haute-Saône), Marcel Laurent Jean-Baptiste Henriot enlisted in the French army on 2 January 1915 and served in the 44e *Régiment d'Artillerie*. Transferring to aviation, he began his training on 29 June 1916 and earned Military Pilot's Brevet No. 4998 at Buc on 1 December. After further training at Avord, Cazaux and Pau, Henriot went to the *Groupe de Division d'Entrainement* on 12 March 1917 and was assigned to *escadrille* N65 a week later. His first victory – an Albatros scout over the Forêt de Pinon at 1740 hrs on 24 April – was also N65's first since 27 December 1916. Henriot's victim was probably Vfw Max Wackwitz of *Jasta* 24, who survived a force-landing at Bignicourt following the melee. Henriot finished the war as an adjutant with six confirmed victories along with the *Médaille Militaire* and *Croix de Guerre* with five palms, and he was subsequently made a *Chevalier de la Légion d'Honneur* on 6 June 1920. He died in Nantes on 19 November 1952.

LEFT
SPAD S126 (RFC serial A.253), photographed at No. 2 Aircraft Depot at Candas on 9 September 1916, was evaluated by No. 60 Sqn. Indeed, the unit's Capt Ernest L. Foot used it to destroy an Albatros two-seater over Avesnes les Bapaume on 28 September. (Leslie Rogers via Jon Guttman)

The first SPAD VII license-built by Mann, Egerton & Co Ltd, N6120 was originally slated for the Royal Naval Air Service but was later allocated to the RFC with the serial A9100. (Johann Visser via Jon Guttman)

saw No. 23 Sqn begin exchanging its mixed bag of FE 2bs and Martinsyde G 100 Elephants for SPAD VIIs.

Meanwhile, arrangements for licence production were made with Mann, Egerton & Co Ltd at Norwich and with L Blériot (Aeronautics) at Brooklands, which later changed its name to Blériot & Spad and moved to Addlestone. In December 1916, the Royal Naval Air Service (RNAS) ordered 50 SPADs from British Nieuport, but in February 1917 that order was changed to SE 5s and then, on 5 March, to Nieuport scouts!

Relatively few British-built SPADs reached the Western Front, most of those serving in Nos. 19 and 23 Sqns being French-built examples. Another 19 SPAD VIIs were allocated to Nos. 30, 63 and 72 Sqns in the Middle East.

The first Russian success in a SPAD VII was achieved over the Western Front on 24 January 1917 when Lt Ivan A. Orlov, temporarily assigned to N3 to acquaint himself with the latest developments in French fighter tactics, scored his fourth victory in concert with Lt Guynemer. Returning to Russia in March, Orlov was flying a Nieuport 17 on 21 May when he scored his fifth victory and on 4 July when he was killed in action.

By early 1917 43 SPAD VIIs had been delivered to the Imperial Russian Air Service, and the Aktionyernoye Obschchestovo Dux plant in Moscow was contracted to build 200. It had only completed about half that number, however, before shortages of Hispano-Suiza engines caused the order to be terminated in early 1918. SPAD VIIs were allotted to several units, but most were sent to the 1st Fighter Group, comprised of the II, IV, XI and XIX Corps Fighter Detachments. Its commander, Rotmistre (cavalry captain) Aleksandr A. Kozakov, scored none of his 20 victories in the SPAD, but several of his pilots did – most notably Praporshik (ensign) Ivan V. Smirnov, who accounted for six of his 11 official successes in it between September 1917 and early 1918.

Although Count Giovanni Caproni had produced the innovative and promising Ca.20 back in 1914, Italy put such disproportionate priority on producing Caproni's tri-motor bombers in accordance with Maggiore Giulio Douhet's theories that it never followed up to develop a successful indigenous land fighter during World War I. Instead, it relied mainly on Nieuport sesquiplanes and later the Italian-commissioned and French-designed Hanriot HD 1, both licence-built by Macchi. In addition, it imported SPAD VIIs, the first of which were issued to *77ª Squadriglia da Caccia* in March 1917. Other Italian units received a few SPADs to complement their normal inventory of Nieuports or Hanriots, but the only others primarily equipped with the type were *71ª* and *91ª Squadriglie*.

Formed on 1 May 1917 with an initial complement of four SPAD VIIs and three Nieuports under the command of Maggiore Guido Tacchini, *91ª Squadriglia* was

This SPAD VII, assigned to *76ª Squadriglia*, was flown in July and August 1917 by Sottotenente Flavio Torello Baracchini, who scored four of his 21 confirmed victories in it before switching to Hanriot HD 1s. (Roberto Gentilli)

built around a veteran cadre drawn from *70ª Squadriglia*, including Capitano Francesco Baracca, whose score then stood at eight. Given command of *91ª Squadriglia* on 6 June, Baracca, like Germany's Manfred von Richthofen and France's Antonin Brocard, sought out talented pilots to form a 'squadron of aces'. Among them were Pier Ruggiro Piccio, who would become Italy's third-ranking ace with 24 victories, Fulco Ruffo di Calabria (20 victories), Ferruccio Ranza (17), Gastone Novelli (8), Luigi Olivari (8) Giuliano Parvis (6), Guido Nardini (6) and Giovanni Sabelli (5). Also similarly to von Richthofen, Baracca gave his pilots considerable leeway in the air, trusting in their ability to know when to fight as a team or to hunt alone.

On 15 August 1917, the first of 15 SPAD VIIs purchased by a Belgian prince was presented to *5e Escadrille*'s sole ace, Sous-Lt Edmond Thieffry, who used it the very next day to shoot down an Albatros two-seater over the Houthulst Forest for his seventh victory. He would score four more victories in SPADs before being brought down by the two-seater crew of Gefr Lunecke and Ltn Sanbold of *Flieger Abteilung* (FA) 227 on 23 February 1918 and taken prisoner. Thieffry's unit, later redesignated *10e Escadrille*, would fly SPAD VIIs and XIIIs for the rest of the war.

The United States bought 189 SPAD VIIs from the French. Prior to it entering the war on 6 April 1917, however, many of its citizens had already flown the type in combat as volunteers. Joining the Foreign Legion, they had either served with the all-American SPA124 'Lafayette' or been farmed out to other *escadrilles* via the Lafayette Flying Corps (LFC). Others, who had furtively passed themselves off as Canadians, had joined the RFC.

On 18 February 1918, SPA124's American personnel transferred into the US Army Air Service (USAS) and were assigned to the 103rd Aero Squadron. They continued to use their SPAD VIIs for a further five months until they were replaced with SPAD XIIIs in July. At about this time the 139th Aero Squadron also began operations with SPAD VIIs, eventually replacing them with XIIIs too.

ALBATROS D III

Since the summer of 1915 German single-seat monoplane tractor fighters – Fokker E I, E II and E III – had dominated the skies over the Western Front. This was not due to outstanding performance so much as to the armament their designer, Anthony Fokker, had incorporated into them – a machine gun whose fire ceased whenever the propeller was in front of it by means of a cam and push rod-operated interrupter gear mechanism. The 'Fokker Scourge' could only go on so long, however, before the Allies found ways to counter it. These ranged from pusher fighters such as Britain's AIRCO DH 2, to tractor fighters with machine guns mounted above the upper wing to fire over the propeller, such as the French Nieuport 11 and 16, or with interrupter gear of their own, such as the British Sopwith Scout (better known as the 'Pup') and the French Nieuport 17 and SPAD VII.

By the time the Battle of the Somme commenced on 1 July 1916, the Allied fighters had virtually retaken command of the sky. Maj Wilhelm Siegert, commander of the *Idflieg* (*Inspektion der Fliegertruppen*, or Inspectorate of Aviation Troops), wrote in outspoken retrospect:

> The start of the Somme battle unfortunately coincided with the low point in the technical development of our aircraft. The unquestioned supremacy we had enjoyed in early 1916 by virtue of our Fokker monoplane fighters shifted over to the enemy's Nieuport, Vickers [a German misidentification of the DH 2] and Sopwith aircraft in March and April.

By October 1916, the aerial balance of power began to shift again. In large degree Siegert attributed the German resurgence to the 'enterprise of Boelcke and his "school" in conjunction with the new Halberstadt D III fighter'. That was partly true, but the Halberstadt D I, D II and D III biplanes had served more of a transitionary role in countering the next generation of Allied fighters while specialised fighter squadrons, or *Jagdstaffeln*, began forming from the smaller *Kampfeinzitzer Kommandos* during August 1916. A more significant fighter arrived the following month at Hptm Martin Zander's *Jasta* 1 and Hptm Oswald Boelcke's *Jasta* 2 in the form of Albatros D Is and D IIs.

Built in the summer of 1916 by the Albatros Werke at Johannesthal, the D I was based on a racing aeroplane developed just before the war by Robert Thelen, supervisor of the Albatros design committee. Its single-bay, twin-spar wing structure was standard for the

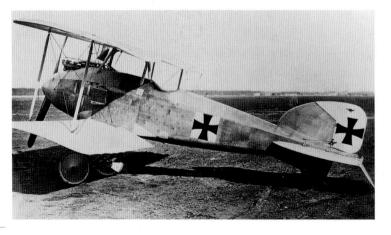

The prototype Albatros D I, shown at Johannisthal early in 1916, features a non-standard exhaust and an unbalanced elevator. (Greg VanWyngarden)

This early Albatros D II shows the improvement in visibility afforded by its lowered upper wing and revised cabane strut arrangement, as well as the drag-producing Windhoff radiators, which would later be replaced with a Teeves und Braun radiator flush with the upper wing. (Greg VanWyngarden)

time, but what distinguished the D I was its streamlined plywood fuselage with a neatly cowled 160hp Mercedes D III engine and a spinner over the propeller. Taking advantage of the more powerful engine, Thelen built the new fighter to carry not one but two synchronised 7.92mm Maxim 08/15 machine guns using Hedtke interrupter gear – a system similar to Fokkers' developed by Albatros' *Werkmeister* – which more than doubled the rate of fire.

Although the Albatros was not as manoeuvrable as most of its opponents, German airmen soon decided that they could live with that, given its superior speed and firepower. Thelen addressed complaints of vision being impeded by the D I's upper wing and trestle-type centre-section struts with the D II, whose lowered upper wing was supported by outward-splayed N-shaped cabane struts. He also subsequently replaced the drag-creating Windhoff radiators on the fuselage sides of the D I and early D IIs with a Teeves und Braun radiator installed flush within the upper wing centre section.

This early Albatros D III of *Jasta* 14, seen running up its engine at Marchais aerodrome in May 1917, features the original positioning of its Teeves und Braun radiator in the upper wing centre section. Pilots complained that it impeded their vision and, if punctured, could leak scalding water in their faces. A flare gun and signal flares are mounted to the right of the cockpit. (Heinz J. Nowarra Album via Greg VanWyngarden)

One of *Jasta* 2's earliest members, Ltn Erwin Böhme, gave his first impression of the new Albatrosen:

Their climb rate and manoeuvrability are astonishing. It is as if they are living, feeling beings that understand what their master wishes. With them, one can dare and achieve anything.

On 16 September Boelcke's *Jasta* 2 received five Albatros D Is and one D II. Flying a D I that same afternoon, Ltn Otto Walter Höhne brought down an FE 2b of No. 11 Sqn.

The next morning, Boelcke inaugurated an innovation more significant than the Albatros – a systematic team effort to achieve local air superiority. Leading five of his men to the front, he spotted 14 British aircraft bombing Marcoing railway station. Staying behind and above, Boelcke sent his charges diving on the enemy formations, which they broke up and then went after individual targets. One of Boelcke's young disciples, Ltn Manfred von Richthofen, sent an FE 2b crashing at Flesquières, killing 2Lts Thomas Rees and Lionel B. F. Morris of No. 11 Sqn, for his first victory. Boelcke and Ltn d R Hans Reimann also downed FE 2bs, while Böhme brought down a Sopwith 1½ Strutter of No. 70 Sqn.

Combining the Albatros D II with the adoption of the 'Boelcke Dicta', *Jasta* 2 headed a general resurgence of German air power over the Western Front, during which Boelcke brought his personal score up to 40 before being killed in a mid-air collision with Böhme (who survived) on 28 October 1916. By 7 January 1917 the *Staffel*, renamed *Jasta* 'Boelcke' in its late commander's honour, was credited with shooting down 87 Allied aircraft in four months – including 16 by von Richthofen, who was awarded the *Orden Pour le Mérite* and given command of *Jasta* 11 at La Brayelle aerodrome. On the very day the unit's new CO arrived, *Jasta* 11 received its first example of a new variation on Albatros' winning formula, the D III.

Inspired by the agility and excellent downward visibility enjoyed by the pilot when flying the French Nieuport 17, whose single-spar lower wing was little more than an aerofoil-section bracing structure for the two-spar upper wing (hence the term sesquiplane or 1½-wing), the Albatros design team tried to achieve the best of both worlds by adopting a similar arrangement for the D II. In June 1916 *Idflieg* ordered three prototypes, which were tested in September. The results were good enough for *Idflieg* to order 400 examples of the sesquiplane in October, and *Jasta* 24 reported receiving its first three D IIIs on 21 December.

Distinguished by wings with a long curving rake at the tips, the D III looked more graceful than the D II with its broad, squared-off wings. Indeed it boasted a superior downward view, better manoeuvrability and a superior rate-of-climb when compared with the early Albatros scouts.

It soon came to light, however, that those qualities came at a price. The D III was heavier and more powerful than the rotary-engined Nieuport (a fully loaded Nieuport 11 weighed 460kg compared to the Albatros D III's 810kg). One consequence of this came to light on 17 January when *Armee Oberkommando* 2 reported four cases of 'Rib fractures and breakage of the leading edge' of the D III's lower wings in the course of turning manoeuvres and diving.

ALBATROS D III

24ft 6in.

9ft 6in.

29ft 6in.

Apparently, the first encounter between the Albatros D III and SPAD VII (offering a vivid display of their differences) occurred on 23 January when Ltn Roland Nauck of *Jasta* 6 reported that as he was diving after a SPAD the lower right wing of his Albatros shed fabric and then the spar itself broke. Although wounded when the SPAD turned the tables on him, Nauck managed to force land in German lines to report what occurred. He was apparently credited as the third victory for Lt Charles de Guibert of N62, who was escorting a Breguet 14A2 of BR213 that had been reconnoitring the Chemin des Dames area in anticipation of the coming offensive. They came under attack by the lone D III, and during the course of the brief melee de Guibert claimed an enemy aeroplane shot down over Fresnes.

On the same day Nauck had his close call, Hptm Manfred von Richthofen opened *Jasta* 11's account by shooting down an FE 8 single-seat pusher fighter, killing 2Lt John Hay of No. 40 Sqn. The next day he brought down an FE 2b of No. 25 Sqn, but was forced to land nearby, explaining in a letter to his mother that 'one of my wings broke during the air battle at 3,000 metres altitude. It was only through a miracle that I reached the ground without going *kaput*'.

Von Richthofen was not exaggerating. That same day, his former unit, *Jasta* 'Boelcke', reported three similar incidents, one of which killed five-victory ace Offstv Leopold Reimann. His confidence in the D III shaken, over the next two months von Richthofen flew a Halberstadt D II, in which he may have scored as many as 11 victories.

On 27 January *Kommandierenden General der Luftstreitskräfte* Ernst von Hoeppner ordered all D IIIs grounded. Responding swiftly to the crisis, Albatros strengthened and braced the D III's lower wing cellule, including sheet metal braces for the front stringers to the lower wing. Those measures sufficed for Hoeppner to lift his ban on 19 February, and D III deliveries resumed in time for the *Jastas* they equipped to face aerial activity that attended Gen Robert Nivelle's spring 1917 offensive.

Flown with aggressiveness and tactical skill by von Richthofen and the pilots he inspired, the D III became the terror of the Western Front in a lopsided three-to-one slaughter of British aircraft that came to be known as 'Bloody April'. Satisfied with this success, *Idflieg* ordered more D IIIs, not only from Johannisthal but from the Ostdeutsche Albatros Werke (OAW) subsidiary in Scheidemühl.

A Roland D II heads a line up of Albatros D IIIs at *Jasta* 27's aerodrome at Ghistelles in May 1917. Upon taking command on 17 May, Ltn Hermann Göring made a point of replacing the last of his unit's Rolands. (Jon Guttman)

TECHNICAL SPECIFICATIONS

SPAD VII

Although accepted early on as a winning formula, the SPAD VII showed ample room for improvement. The most irritating problem initially afflicting the aircraft was its radiator. As SPAD contracted production to different factories, shortages in copper, brass and other materials resulted in each constructor devising a different radiator. Their inconsistent quality hindered manufacture and caused maintenance problems until March 1917, when Bonfils et Laval's octagonal radiator was standardised as being most resistant to engine vibration. Even that type, however, seemed to fall short both in keeping the motor from overheating in the summer and allowing it to warm up in the winter.

A variety of measures were taken by frontline units to address the radiator problem by increasing or reducing the airflow over its surface. Two different cowlings were sometimes kept on hand – one with a small aperture for winter and a wider one for summer. If both were not available, a section of shaped sheet metal, solid or slatted, might be fitted over the radiator within the wider cowl in cold weather. If the wider one was not available during a warm period, holes were sometimes fretted into the front of the narrow cowlings. The ultimate solution to the problem was to adjust the airflow, and the arrangements experimented with included a circular set of blinds that could be rotated to increase or decrease radiator exposure. Finally, a set of seven vertical, adjustable shutter bars became standard.

In November 1916 a SPAD VII's wings were modified with reduced span and greater chord, but the resulting effect on performance proved insufficient to justify

An early SPAD VII marked with the twin red bands of N112 and an interesting dragon marking chosen by the pilot also shows the narrow cold-weather radiator cowling that was often exchanged for a wider one during warmer months.
(Greg VanWyngarden)

further experimentation after December. A flatter planform was tested in February 1917 but was likewise abandoned.

More favourable improvements were the replacement of the aluminium fuselage bracing components with steel ones, stronger steel plate engine bearers and more internal bracing of the fuselage framework with steel cables. The rear undercarriage legs of some SPAD VIIs were fitted with racks for 22lb Anelite bombs for the ground attack role.

While Georges Guynemer was among the SPAD VII's most zealous advocates, by the same token he was most influential in demanding improvements to the basic formula. In December 1916 he sent a letter to Béchereau explaining that 'the 150hp SPAD is not a match for the Halberstadt. Although the Halberstadt is probably no faster, it climbs better. Consequently, it has the overall advantage. More speed is needed – possibly the airscrew could be improved'.

Marc Birkigt was already dealing with the power issue. On 11 June 1916, Hispano-Suiza successfully bench-tested the new 8B V8 engine, which could produce 208hp at 2,000rpm at ground level, and used a spur reduction gear to transfer that power to the propeller. After testing the 8B in a SPAD VII, Béchereau concluded that a somewhat larger, more robust airframe would be required to accommodate it. The larger SPAD 13.C1 or XIII, which was ordered into production in February 1917, also featured rounded wingtips, forward-staggered cabane struts with a frontal bracing wire and twin 0.303-in Vickers machine guns with 380 rounds each.

In addition to developing the new geared Hispano-Suiza 8B, Birkigt souped up the SPAD VII's original engine by increasing the compression ratio from 4.7:1 to 5.3:1. The result was an increase in output to 180hp at 1,800rpm, with a full-throttle capacity of 204hp, the potential of which was exploited by a reduction in propeller pitch.

The first SPAD VII fitted with the new 8Ab engine, S254, was presented to Guynemer in January 1917. By the end of the month his score had risen to 30, and he was delightedly referring to the 180hp SPAD as his *mitrailleuse volante* (flying machine gun). He would score 19 of his victories in S254 and, just as significantly, its engine was never changed. After finally being retired from frontline service, historic S254 survived to be preserved and displayed at the *Musée de l'Air et l'Espace* at Le Bourget.

SPAD VII COCKPIT

1. Water and auxiliary fuel pipes
2. 0.303-in Vickers machine gun
3. Charging handle cable
4. Radiator cap
5. Windscreen
6. Le Crétien gunsight
7. Ammunition discharge chute
8. Ammunition feed chute
9. Magneto switch

10. Air pump emergency shut-off
11. Fuel tank selector
12. Air pump selector/air pressure release
13. Air pressure regulator
14. Speedometer
15. Altimeter
16. Oil temperature gauge
17. Tachometer
18. Water temperature gauge

19. Oil pressure gauge
20. Throttle and fuel regulator
21. Compass
22. Rudder bar
23. Control column with trigger
24. Fuel gauge
25. Seat
26. Starting magneto
27. Hand-operated fuel pump

SPAD VII				
Dimensions				
Wingspan (upper)	25ft 8in			
Wingspan (lower)	24ft 10in			
Chord (upper)	4ft 7.5in			
Chord (lower)	4ft 2in			
Wing Area	58.563 sq ft			
Dihedral	0 degrees			
Length	19ft 11in			
Height	7ft 3in			
Armament	one 0.303-in Vickers machine gun two 22lb Anelite bombs			
Weight (lb)				
Empty	1,102			
Loaded	1,554			
Performance				
Engine	150hp Hispano-Suiza 8Aa		180hp Hispano-Suiza 8Ab	
Maximum speed (mph)				
6,100ft (2,000m)	116		132	
9,150ft (3,000m)	112		127	
12,200ft (4,000m)	108		124	
Climb to	min	sec	min	sec
6,100ft (2,000m)	6	40	4	40
9,150ft (3,000m)	11	20	8	10
Service Ceiling (feet)	18,045		21,500	
Endurance	2 hrs 40 min		1 hr 30 min	

By April 1917 the 180hp Hispano-Suiza 8Ab had been standardised as the SPAD VII engine, although production still had to catch up with the lower-powered airframes in frontline service. The performance the 8Ab gave the SPAD VII combined with the superior reliability its direct drive had over the geared 150hp 8Aa engine kept the VII competitive to the end of the war. Although its single machine gun was a weakness in the war's last two years, many French units kept a complement of SPAD VIIs in case their better-armed, more powerful XIIIs suffered breakdowns in the field.

Adj André Martenot de Cordoux, who was the first member of *escadrille* N94 to receive a SPAD VII in September 1917, remembered it as being less manoeuvrable than the Nieuport 24, but nimble enough to hold its own against its German opponents in a dogfight if necessary, and superior to most others for making a diving, hit-and-run attack. Even after he was issued a SPAD XIII in the spring of 1918, he chose to keep a VII as well:

I would fly regular missions in the SPAD XIII in order to keep formation for the standard SPAD XIII was faster than the VII. When all SPADs returned, I would use my VII between patrols, on my own individual flights. Despite the single gun and lower speed, it was more manoeuvrable than the XIII and, frankly, the closeness of our combats rendered speed less important.

Typifying the impression the SPAD VII made on members of the two RFC units to fly it over the Western Front was that recalled by William M. Fry (who was assigned to command 'B' Flight in No. 23 Sqn on 20 October 1917) in his memoir *Air of Battle*:

The SPAD VII flown by Sous-Lt Pierre Besançon of SPA163 undergoes maintenance in the spring of 1918. This fighter displays the defininitive adjustable radiator shutter arrangement, with the slats fully open for hot weather. At this point in the war, the higher-compression Hispano-Suiza 8Ab engine, which boosted output from 150hp to 180hp, was standard and kept the SPAD VII's performance competitive with its German opposition. (SHAA B87.3759)

The squadron's machines were French SPAD single-seater scouts with the 180hp Hispano-Suiza direct-drive engine, the propeller being driven straight off the crankshaft. Some of the engines in the squadron were French, built under licence, some English, also built under licence by the Wolseley Motor Company, and an occasional engine built by the Hispano-Suiza Company itself. These last were much sought after by pilots. Of those built under licence, it was generally thought by the pilots that the French Peugeots were the better, the English engines being less reliable, but we understood that the plant for making them had been set up in great haste and it was a marvel to have produced them at all in the time. They improved as teething troubles were overcome. Having flown SPADs for a few hours at London Colney, I started operational flying immediately.

Our SPADs at that time had one Vickers gun firing forward through the propeller and built in under the engine cowling between the 'V' of the cylinder blocks, and with a quite reliable French interrupter gear. It was a beautifully built aeroplane, very strong, which made it rather heavy, and it was reputed to have the gliding angle of a brick when the engine was throttled back or shut off. For this reason it was not popular with some RFC pilots.

There were two pairs of struts on each side between the wings, and all flying and landing wires were duplicated. These were of cable wire, about an inch apart, with strips of wood fairing grooved between each pair for streamlining. Both features were unusual in scout machines, but what little was lost in speed was made up in strength. Anyhow, they were as fast as anything the RFC possessed. Aileron flaps on the top wings only made lateral control rather sloppy, but most of us who flew the SPAD liked the machine, despite its general unpopularity in the RFC.

The SPAD was comfortable to sit in, with a roomy seat and plenty of elbow room on each side, and with a well-padded cockpit fairing at precisely the right height to enable one to look over the side downwards behind the trailing edge of the bottom wings. The all-round view downward was not very good, but somehow the view behind the bottom wings afforded an excellent field for picking up machines flying below, and a slight turn either way increased the field of view tremendously.

The view above was perfect as one's head was a little way behind and not far below the level of the centre section and top planes. It was a bit of a hazard that the pilot's seat was the petrol tank, specially adapted and shaped for this purpose, with a wicker seat and cushion on top. A few bullets through the tank, especially if there were a tracer or two among them, betokened an end in those days of no parachutes and 40 or more gallons of petrol immediately beneath one's bottom. But we didn't think about it as that would have done no good, and anyhow, it didn't make much difference where the petrol was if a tracer went through it – the result was the same.

SPAD VII FUSELAGE GUN

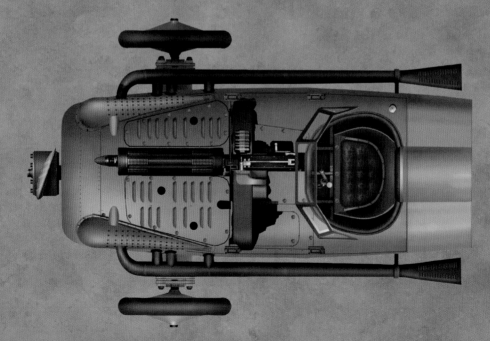

The French SPAD VII was armed with a single 0.303-in Vickers machine gun, synchronised using mechanical interrupter gear developed by Marc Birkigt of Hispano-Suiza. The weapon fired 600 rounds of belt-fed ammunition.

ALBATROS D III

While reporting on the performance of the German fighters – by then primarily Albatros D IIIs – in the summer of 1917, Rittm Manfred von Richthofen addressed the aeroplane's characteristics aside from its lower wing issues. One critical factor in a fighter's success, he declared, was its ability to not lose height in a tight turn at high altitudes, and he flatly stated 'This is not the case with the Albatros D III. It is the aeroplane's chief drawback'. Regarding lateral control, he added, 'the ailerons of the Albatros D III are not entirely effective. Aileron control is the main requirement of a fighter'. The Baron found rudder control good, however, and the elevator 'very pleasant'.

Another important trait was visibility, which von Richthofen said must not be 'encumbered above, below and to the side'. In that respect he rated the D III as 'good'. As to its ability to dive 1,000 metres or more and pull out with absolute safety, von Richthofen declared that that was not always the case even on the reinforced D III.

It is interesting to note how similar in essence von Richthofen's candid appraisal of the Albatros D III was to those of Allied pilots who got to evaluate captured specimens. Capt Cecil A. Lewis flew one in which Ltn Georg Simon of *Jasta* 11 had been brought down and captured on 4 June 1917, and he gave his impressions in his memoir, *Farewell to Wings*:

ALBATROS D III FUSELAGE GUNS

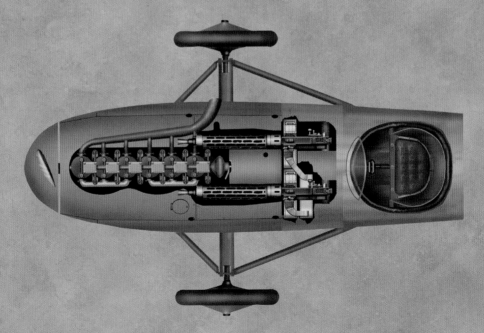

The Albatros D III was armed with twin 7.92mm LMG 08/15 machine guns with 550 rounds of ammunition each. Both the D III's Hetke interrupter gear and the improved Semmler gear that synchronised the guns on later OAW-built machines were developed by Albatros factory Werkmeisters.

An Albatros D III built by the Ostdeutsche Albatros Werke displays the later model's D V-style rudder. Distrust in the Albatros D V and its intended successors, together with the need to fulfil the *Amerika Programm*, resulted in OAW getting a last order for D IIIs in September 1917. This aeroplane was delivered to one such *Amerika Programm* unit, *Jasta* 43. (Johann Visser via Jon Guttman)

I don't know what it was made of, but it gave the impression of *papier maché*. However, being rounded out like a fish, it was far more roomy and the whole machine seemed larger because of this cavernous cockpit. The engine, water-cooled, had a neat radiator in the centre-section, but it was big and heavy. In fact the Germanic temperament showed up all along. The machine was sluggish, strong, reliable and determined. It had none of the feeling of lightness and grace that our aircraft had. Very few pilots could take over the controls of a strange type and really measure up its capabilities in an hour or so, so it is probable we never really stretched it, but I am certain of one thing. To throw an Albatros around in the air was hard work, and it would have made you sweat in a dogfight.

Even while the strengthened D III was showing its merits Albatros worked on a successor with a lightened airframe and even more streamlined fuselage. Approved for production by *Idflieg* on 21 April 1917, the aircraft began to reach frontline units as the Albatros D V, but it soon proved to offer a scant improvement in performance, while displaying a more marked tendency for the lower wing to vibrate and suffer structural failure in a dive.

Groundcrews as well as the Albatros Werke itself again took steps to reinforce the wings, including adding extra bracing wires or a small auxiliary strut from the lower front of the V-shaped interplane strut to the lower wing – the latter was also sometimes added to D IIIs as well. Even then, more than a few pilots balked at accepting even reinforced D Vs. Von Richthofen, for one, stated his preference for the D III over the 'lousy' D V that summer. Oblt Rudolf Berthold was still flying a D III when he commanded *Jasta* 18 as late as October 1917. *Idflieg* agreed, and in a report on 24 July it stated:

The Albatros D III is more robustly constructed than the D V. The D V is merely regarded as a lightened D III. The performance of both is equal. The D V will not be manufactured further, only the D III.

By then, however, the German drive to double its fighter strength through the *Amerika Programm* had left Albatros committed to D V production. Its engineers' efforts to correct the new fighter's shortcomings led in August to the D Va, whose higher compression Mercedes D IIIa engine compensated for the beefed-up fuselage and wing structure. Even then Albatros hedged its bets by having its OAW subsidiary continue building D IIIs. When production ceased in September, Albatros had built a total of 508 D IIIs, including prototypes, and OAW had produced another 838.

As with the SPAD VII, the Albatros D III underwent some radiator refinement. A hit on the centrally mounted upper wing radiator risked showering scalding water on the pilot. There had also been complaints from the frontline that the pipes connecting the radiator to the engine interfered with gun aiming. After the first 306 were delivered, future D IIIs were built with the radiator offset to the right.

With the advent of warmer weather, on 29 April 1917 *Jasta* 24 reported that four of its fighters had had to return after ten minutes due to the water in their radiators boiling over. After improvised larger or more efficient radiators had been trialled in the frontline, Daimler solved the problem once and for all when its radiator, boasting hexagonal cooling tubes, was fitted to two D IIIs from 4 June.

Some OAW-built D IIIs were strengthened to accommodate an operational load of 235kg (518lb), rather than the standard 135 kg (298 lb). These specially modified machines carried twin radiators on the upper wing for shipment to German and Turkish units in the hotter environs of Mesopotamia and Palestine.

Albatros D III		
Dimensions		
Wingspan (upper)	29ft 6in	
Wingspan (lower)	28ft 11in	
Chord (upper)	4ft 11in	
Chord (lower)	3ft 7in	
Wing Area	225 sq ft	
Dihedral	2 degrees (lower wing only)	
Length	24ft 6in	
Height	9ft 6in	
Armament	two 7.92mm LMG 08/15s	
Weight (lb)		
Empty	1,484	
Loaded	2,002	
Performance		
Engine	160hp Mercedes D III	
Maximum speed (mph)	102	
Climb to	min	sec
3,050ft (1,000m)	2	30
6,100ft (2,000m)	6	0
9,150ft (3,000m)	11	0
12,200ft (4,000m)	17	0
15,250ft (6,000m)	24	30
Service Ceiling (feet)	18,000	
Endurance	2 hrs	

EXPERIMENTS

In November 1916 *Idflieg* ordered five Albatros D IIIs fitted with 'wrapped' fuselages. These seem to have been made of interwoven strips, as patented by the A. Gelpel company. Two such fuselages, one bare and the other fabric covered, were exposed to the elements for three weeks and then tested at Adlershof on 4-5 July 1917. Both failed to hold up to the load requirements, and an attempt to reinforce them with an interior framework raised their weight to that of the standard fuselage, nullifying the advantage sought in using them.

ALBATROS D III COCKPIT

1. Engine coolant pipes
2. Windscreen
3. 7.92mm LMG 08/15 machine guns
4. Auxiliary throttle handle
5. Tachometer
6. Spent ammunition chutes
7. Mounting bar for guns and instruments
8. Altimeter
9. Air pressure selector handle
10. Air pressure selector
11. Air pump selector valve

12. Spark control handle
13. Throttle handle
14. Spent ammunition can
15. Ammunition belt containers in front of spent ammunition can
16. Control column
17. Fuel pressure gauge
18. Starting magneto
19. Magneto switch key
20. Fuel pressure gauge valve control
21. Fuel quantity gauge

22. Water pump greaser
23. Rudder control bar
24. Hand-operated air pump
25. Magnetic compass
26. Adjustable leather-padded aluminium seat
27. Machine gun buttons
28. Control column grip
29. Rearview mirror
30. Radiator control handle

The Albatros D III entered combat using Hedtke interrupter gear, which was modified to increase the rate of fire by a third in January 1917. Later in the year another Albatros engineer, Werkmeister Semmler, devised an improved system that was used until August, when the Anthony Fokker-owned Flugzeug-Waffen Fabrik *Zentral* sychronisation mechanism was standardised for all Albatros fighters.

The D III served as a testbed for various weaponry and equipment. Ltn Rudolf Nebel of *Jasta* 5 mounted two tubes under the wings to fire four signal rockets at enemy aircraft, but one exploded prematurely and Nebel was fortunate to survive with burns. On 10-15 October 1917, an engine-driven *Motor-Maschinen-Gewehr*, designed by Ober-Ingenieur Harald Wolff at the Siemens-Schuckert Werke, was demonstrated on the D III, giving a rate of fire of 800 rounds per minute – this was later raised to 1,350. The weapon was field-tested on D Vas early in 1918 but not adopted for production.

In December 1916 Ltn Rudolf Hohberg of *Flieger Abteilung* (A) 263 proposed using a fighter for high-speed reconnaissance and mounted cameras in a D II in February 1917. He later mounted one in D III 1991/16 (formerly flown by Ltn Eduard Lübbert of *Jasta* 11), and on 25 May took 300 strip photographs of the Arras sector. In spite of such success, the Germans never adopted his idea and his last flight took place on 21 August.

In early 1917, the German Navy Airship Command tried mounting a fighter on its Zeppelins to provide them with a ready escort. On 25-26 January, D III 3066/16, fitted with a downward-directed engine exhaust to reduce the fire risk to the airship, was taken up by Zeppelin L 35 and released from its harness. Although this first test of a 'parasite fighter' was a success, problems with the water-cooled engine freezing at high altitudes and the question of landing if released over England or the North Sea led to the project being, if one may pardon the unavoidable pun, dropped.

COMPARATIVE IMPRESSIONS

The Albatros D III's arrival early in 1917 was greeted with high hopes, followed by alarm when wing failures occurred. Its performance with reinforced wing cellules during 'Bloody April' restored morale to a guarded optimism, but taking the SPAD VII's measure left the *Jagdflieger* with few illusions as to how the two fighters matched up.

Ltn Ernst Udet of *Jasta* 15, whose memoir *Mein Fliegerleben* included a tense account of his one-on-one dogfight with Capt Georges Guynemer on 15 June 1917, which ended with his guns jammed and Guynemer chivalrously sparing him with what Udet swore was a parting salute, did not mince words about the opposition. 'Across from us', he wrote, 'the elite of the French air service is deployed. They fly the single-seat SPAD with the 180 Hispano. A fast, agile machine, superior to our Shark (Roland D II *Haifisch*) and Albatros, especially in the dive, when our wing planes begin to quake so we fear they'll tear off in the air. The more sturdy SPAD takes these stresses much better'.

Udet's comments make for interesting reading when compared with those of Capt Albert Deullin in his essay on *Fighter Tactics*.

The 180hp SPAD will outfly the 160hp Albatros both in level flight or in a dive at a modest angle with the motor on, but in a steep dive the Albatros, with its heavy motor, will go at least as fast as any other machine.

Curiously, Deullin made no mention of structural problems with the D III's wing in a 'steep dive'.

Another personal appraisal appeared in 'The Latest Types of Fighting Aeroplanes', a photo essay in an American illustrated magazine written by Carroll Dana Winslow, an LFC volunteer who had served in MF44 and N112. Under a photograph of a SPAD VII, Winslow wrote:

The latest type of French fighting aeroplane. The wing surface is less than 18 square yards. It is very fast and efficient, but when it meets the 'Albatross', unless the pilot is very expert and experienced, it has generally found its master and the fight ends disastrously for us.

An Albatros D III (Oef) – probably 153.06 – of Hptm Godwin Brumowski's *Flik* 41/J has its cowling removed to show the Austro-Daimler engine and the protruding tubes for the twin Schwarzlose machine guns, which – unlike on most German aircraft – were installed within the cockpit, impeding the pilot's ability to reach them in the event of a jam. (Greg VanWyngarden)

OEFFAG D IIIs

Even while the Germans were having trouble with their Albatros V-strutters, their Austro-Hungarian allies were starting to manufacture their own D IIIs. Ironically, in so doing they managed to develop a variant superior to any sesquiplane Albatros produced, or, for that matter, any fighter Austria-Hungary's own aeroplane builders fielded in the course of the war.

Established at Steinfeld aerodrome on the outskirts of Wiener Neustadt in March 1915, the Oesterreichische Flugzeugfabrik Allgemeine Gesellschaft, or Oeffag, began building two-seaters and flying boats, but with the success of the Albatros D II on the Western Front it applied to manufacture that as well. By the time the licence was signed on 4 December 1916 the D III was also in production, so the Austrian firm manufactured 20 D IIs and 30 D IIIs. All bore the number code 53, and ultimately four D IIIs replaced an identical number of D IIs when production of the latter fighter was completed in March 1917.

Numbered 53.01 to 53.16, the Oeffag D IIs differed from their German prototypes by having 185hp Austro-Daimler engines in place of the 160hp Mercedes units, along with separate exhausts, a different radiator centrally

mounted on the upper wing, a ten-centimetre increase in the depth of the wings and differences in cockpit and ventral fin shapes. Armament consisted of a single 8mm Schwarzlose MG 16 machine gun installed within the fuselage, with a prolonged barrel extending to the right of the engine. First test flown in January 1917, Oeffag D IIs reached *Fliegerkompagnien*, or *Fliks*, in May, and were initially assigned to the Eastern Front.

The first D III was completed in February 1917, but reports of warping and wing failure in the German D IIIs led Oeffag to hold off deliveries until it had reinforced the airframe. All strut contact points in particular were strengthened before flight-testing began at Fischamend on 17 May. As a result, after the Oeffag-built D IIIs were released for service in June, only one case of vibration in the lower wing was reported.

Besides being more robust than German Albatros D IIIs, the Oeffags displayed superior speed, climb, manoeuvrability and infinitely safer flight characteristics than the Hansa-Brandenburg D Is they had begun to supplant in the *Fliegerkompagnien*. The principal pilots' criticism concerned their guns being buried in the fuselage below eye level, which did not improve the aerodynamics of the fuselage and made them hard to clear in the event of a jam.

After initially producing its fighters with a single gun, Oeffag began standardising around twin weapons in February 1917, when the KuK *Kriegsministerium* ordered another 61 D IIIs (serialed 153.01 to 153.61) to be powered by 200hp Austro-Daimler engines. The 153 version was flight tested in December 1917 and despatched to the front soon after.

Adapting interrupter gear to the Austrian Schwarzlose machine gun, with its retarded blowback, proved more difficult than for the German LMG 08/15. Anthony Fokker tried, but before he succeeded Ltn Otto Bernatzik, the technical officer for *Flik* 8, devised interrupter gear that was actuated by an exhaust rocker arm at every second propeller revolution. In the spring of 1916 this was installed in Hansa-Brandenburg C Is and subsequently in some D Is. Later, Oblt Eduard Zaparka developed interrupter gear for the Hiero engine that would accommodate twin machine guns, albeit at every fourth engine revolution. Daimler produced one that doubled the Zaparka gear's rate of fire and in October 1917, Oblt Guido Priesel came up with a variation on Fokker's cam system that was superior to the Daimler gear and became standard on Oeffag Albatros D IIIs in 1918.

Stfw Frigyes Hefty, a Hungarian pilot in *Flik* 42/J, gave a typical appraisal of the new fighter:

> The 200hp D III was an aeroplane of an excellent design, perfectly balanced and especially fit for aerobatics. Its climbing capacity equalled that of Hanriots and Camels, but its horizontal speed was lower than that of SPADs.

Instances of spinners coming off and damaging the aeroplanes led many Austro-Hungarian D III pilots to remove them, and in its 153.112-153.211 production batch Oeffag dispensed with the spinner entirely. Altering the design with a rounded nose behind the airscrew actually increased speed by 9kmh. The 253 series featured a

An Albatros D III (Oef) of the 253 series belonging to *Flik* 63/J shows the type's rounded, spinnerless nose. Also of interest is the Austrian placement of crosses on the wing undersides. (Greg VanWyngarden)

still-further strengthened airframe whose weight was offset by a 225hp Austro-Daimler engine. Later, production versions also repositioned the machine guns above the cowling in front of the cockpit, as on most German fighters.

Able to reach a maximum speed of 125mph, the 253 series D III was the highest-performing Albatros sesquiplane of the war, Austrian or German, and its pilots agreed that it was superior to their indigenously produced Phönix D II and Berg D I fighters. Production of the 253 series totalled 260, however, and Oeffag's entire D III output came to just 586. In the same period, Albatros produced about 900 D Vs and 1,012 D Vas, to which OAW added another 600 D Vas. The superior quality of Austro-Hungary's Albatros D IIIs came at a stiff price in terms of quantity.

Oeffag D III	Series 53		Series 153		Series 253	
Weight (lb)						
Empty	1,530		1,560		1,579	
Useful load	331		331		331	
Loaded	2,127		2,125		2,215	
Engine	185hp Austro-Daimler		200hp Austro-Daimler		225hp Austro-Daimler	
Maximum speed	108mph		116mph		125mph	
Climb to	min	sec	min	sec	min	sec
3,050ft	3	20	2	35	2	15
6,100ft	7	10	6	34	5	15
9,150ft	14	30	11	21	9	15
12,200ft	18	16	15	15	-	-
15,250ft	31	42	20	15	-	-

THE STRATEGIC SITUATION

FRANCE AND ITALY IN 1917

For Germany, 1916 had been an exasperating year of failed offensives and defensive crises. It began in February with Gen Erich von Falkenhayn's attack on Verdun, which degenerated into a static war of attrition that ended in December with little to show for the hundreds of thousands of casualties suffered on both sides. On 1 July the British launched an offensive along the Somme River, only to suffer another horrendous bloodletting with negligible reward. In the east, however, Russian Gen Aleksei Brusilov's offensive from 4 June to 7 July so badly mauled the Central Powers – particularly the Austro-Hungarian First Army – as to necessitate a shift in forces, including the transfer of the Turkish XV Corps to Eastern Europe, to avert collapse.

Amid all that, on 29 August Falkenhayn was replaced as Chief of the General Staff by Paul Ludwig Hans Anton von Beneckendorff und von Hindenburg. Together with his chief of staff Gen Erich Ludendorff, Hindenburg turned Germany's original war aim, which in 1914 had envisioned defeating the Western powers first and then concentrating on Russia, completely on its head. Their strategy for 1917 was founded upon a defensive stance in the west while striving for a decisive victory over Russia, which in spite of Brusilov's victory was showing promising signs (to the Germans) of political, economic and moral strain.

In order to resist the next succession of French and British offensives more effectively, between 21 February and the end of March 1917 the Germans carried out Operation *Alberich* – a general withdrawal across France. The more compact defences in depth that resulted, running from Arras along the river Scarpe to the Chemin des

Dames ridge, were collectively dubbed the *Siegfried Stellung* by the Germans but more widely known among the Allies as the Hindenburg Line.

Paralleling the German army's defensive attitude, the *Luftstreitskräfte*'s new *Jagdstaffeln* likewise guarded the airspace over the fortified trenchlines and strongpoints in order to make the most of its limited resources in countering the Allies' overall numerical superiority. During the Verdun campaign Oswald Boelcke had devised a system of stationing fighter aeroplanes at aerodromes near the front so that they could respond to reports of Allied activity with a minimum expenditure of time and fuel. His disciples, most notably Manfred von Richthofen, expanded upon Boelcke's tactical principles, aided by the generally westerly direction of the wind, which worked to the disadvantage of Allied aircraft trying to get back over the lines. To paraphrase von Richthofen, if the enemy insisted on coming to one's shop, why go out looking for customers?

Even while the Germans reorganised for the defence, the new French commander-in-chief, Gen Robert Nivelle, planned a grand artillery-supported offensive northward along the Aisne River, in conjunction with assaults by the British First and Third armies eastward from Arras, to be launched in April 1917. As had been the case during the Battle of the Somme, Gen Trenchard employed the RFC as aggressively as the Germans husbanded their air assets sparingly, despatching his fighter squadrons on regular offensive patrols (OPs) whether for a specific purpose (as the French did) or simply to, as he put it, 'reduce the Hun to a proper state of mind'.

Given the tactical advantages possessed by the *Jagdstaffeln* early in 1917, Trenchard's policy played into the enemy's hands. Even amid the aerial slaughter of 'Bloody April' though, the RNAS gave the Germans cause for concern with its Sopwith Triplane. The RFC also introduced the SE 5 and the Bristol F 2A Fighter early in April, and although neither aeroplane made a significant impression on the Germans at the time, their improved descendants, the SE 5a and the F 2B, soon would.

Also of concern to the Germans was the United States' declaration of war on 6 April, bringing the self-proclaimed birthplace of the aeroplane and an industrial power of vast potential into the conflict. While German aeroplane firms strove to match or surpass the new Allied fighters, the *Luftstreitskräfte* also had to take quantity into consideration.

One consequence was the launching on 23 June of the *Amerika Programm*, which doubled the available units – on paper at least. To give substance to the newly formed *Jastas*, for at least six months the *Kommandierte General der Luftstreitskräfte* (*Kogenluft*) could not afford to interrupt the manufacture of fighters of proven design. That proven design was the Albatros D III, its 'lightened' offspring, the D V, and the later, sturdier but basically similar D Va. Until production of a successor reached full tempo, the *Jagdflieger* would have to do their best with them.

The Nivelle Offensive ended on 20 April with 187,000 French casualties for negligible gains. The British Expeditionary Force (BEF) had suffered 158,660 casualties when the advance from Arras ceased on 17 May, its only major success being the brilliant – by World War I Western Front standards – capture of Vimy Ridge by the Canadian Corps between 9 and 12 April. With the French army exhausted and riddled with mutinies, the BEF tried to keep up the pressure by overrunning the salient around Messines Ridge between 7 and 14 June. After that, the *Luftstreitskräfte*

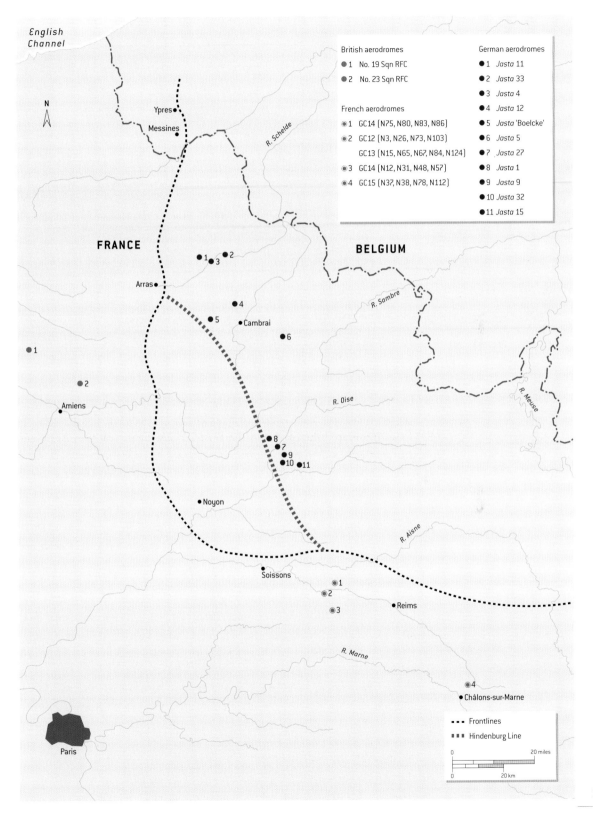

English
Channel

N

FRANCE

Ypres
Messines

R. Schelde

British aerodromes
● 1   No. 19 Sqn RFC
● 2   No. 23 Sqn RFC

French aerodromes
◉ 1   GC14 (N75, N80, N83, N86)
◉ 2   GC12 (N3, N26, N73, N103)
       GC13 (N15, N65, N67, N84, N124)
◉ 3   GC14 (N12, N31, N48, N57)
◉ 4   GC15 (N37, N38, N78, N112)

German aerodromes
● 1   Jasta 11
● 2   Jasta 33
● 3   Jasta 4
● 4   Jasta 12
● 5   Jasta 'Boelcke'
● 6   Jasta 5
● 7   Jasta 27
● 8   Jasta 1
● 9   Jasta 9
● 10 Jasta 32
● 11 Jasta 15

BELGIUM

● 1 ● 3 ● 2
Arras

● 4
● 5   ● Cambrai
          ● 6

R. Sambre

● 1

● 2
Amiens

R. Oise

R. Meuse

● 8
● 7
● 9
● 10 ● 11

● Noyon

R. Aisne

Soissons

◉ 1
◉ 2
◉ 3

● Reims

R. Marne

◉ 4
● Châlons-sur-Marne

- - - Frontlines
▪▪▪ Hindenburg Line

Paris

0   20 miles
0   20 km

finally began doing what the French had already done with their *Groupes de Combat* and the British with their wings – gather and coordinate their *Jasta* operations.

'During a defensive battle', Rittm von Richthofen declared, 'it is best that each *Gruppe* [army group] is assigned a *Jagdgruppe*. This *Jagdgruppe* is not bound strictly to the *Gruppe* sector, but its main purpose is to enable the working aircrews to perform their function and, in exceptional cases, to provide them with immediate protection.

'Moreover the AOK [*Armee Oberkommando*] has at its disposal a large number of *Jagdstaffeln* (*Geschwadern*), which by all means must be allowed to hunt freely and whose mission throughout is dedicated to stopping the enemy flight operations. These AOK forces should not be dispersed for protection flights, escort flights or defensive patrols. Their mission is determined by the *Geschwader-Kommandeur* according to the instructions of the *KoFl* [*Kommandeur der Flieger*]'.

While local units were coordinated as *Jagdgruppen*, their makeup varied according to the situation. Von Richthofen commanded the first of the more permanent and flexible *Jagdgeschwader* on 24 June when *Jastas* 4, 6, 10 and his own 11 were officially combined into JG I. That formation was soon travelling to Flanders when the British opened a new offensive there on 31 July, initiating an agonising 'slugfest' known both as the Third Battle of Ypres and Passchendaele. While fighting on the ground dragged on until 6 November, JG I's tendency to motor from one hot spot to another, the colourful *Staffel* and individual markings on its aeroplanes and the star quality of its pilots earned it the sobriquet – and notoriety – of the 'Flying Circus'.

A final British push toward Cambrai, involving the first massed use of tanks, was launched on 20 November. After making some encouraging initial gains it bogged down, and on the 30th German counterattacks stabilised the front once more.

By the end of 1917 things were looking up for the Central Powers. Romania, which had entered the war on the Allied side on 27 August 1916, had been practically neutralised by January 1917, with most of its southern regions occupied – including Ploesti, from which the Germans had appropriated a million tons of vitally needed oil by the end of the war. In the Battle of Caporetto, fought on 25-26 October 1917, the Austro-Hungarians, bolstered by a substantial German land and air contingent, threw the Italian army into routed retreat to the Piave River. The breakout of the Russian Revolution on 7 November 1917 (25 October on the Julian calendar that was still used by the Russians at the time) eventually led to Bolshevik capitulation on 3 March 1918, freeing up thousands of German soldiers for service on the Western Front. Only in the Middle East was the news bad, as the British advanced steadily in Palestine and Mesopotamia.

In the early months of 1918 the Germans withdrew forces from Russia and Italy and laid plans for a massive offensive on the Western Front, aimed at knocking France out of the war and forcing the Allies to negotiate an end to the conflict on terms favourable to the Central Powers before the Americans could play a significant role.

By the time the *Kaiserschlacht* was launched on 21 March, the Albatros D III had been relegated to a tertiary role in Germany's fighter force, but the Oeffag version was becoming a mainstay of Austro-Hungary's. Problems with the geared Hispano-Suiza 8B engine in the SPAD XIII meant that the SPAD VII remained an essential element in France's *escadrilles de chasse*, but new British designs were eclipsing it in the RFC squadrons, as was the Macchi-built Hanriot HD 1 in Italy's *squadriglie da caccia*.

SPAD VII S331, bearing the new 'Sioux Indian head' insignia of N124 'Lafayette', shares Cachy aerodrome with an older Nieuport 21 still marked with the unit's original 'Seminole' emblem on 1 May 1917. Following their country's declaration of war against Germany on 6 April, N124's American volunteer pilots proudly flew the 'Stars & Stripes' at their airfields. As part of *Groupe de Combat* 13, N124 was active in Gen Robert Nivelle's Aisne offensive, mainly from Ham aerodrome. (SHAA B83.3461)

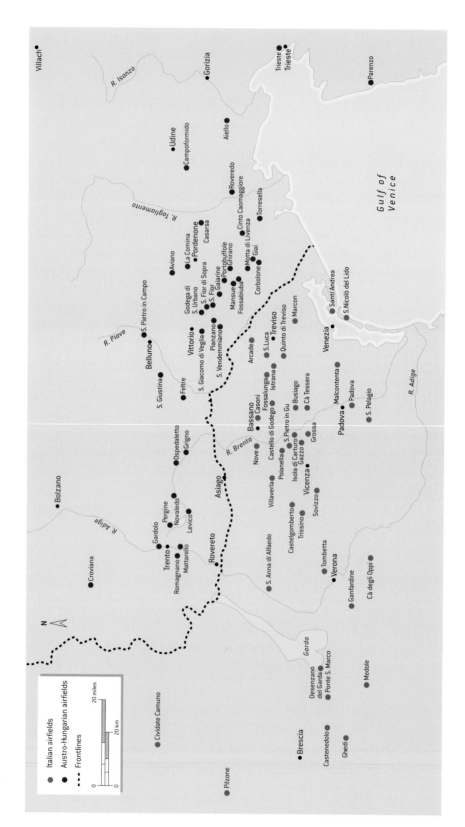

Italian SPAD units held their own against the German *Jagdstaffeln* and the Austro-Hungarian Oeffag Albatros D III-equipped *Jagdfliegerkompagnien* during the Battle of Caporetto in October 1917, but were caught up in the general rout of the Italian army. Nevertheless, by early November the Italians had retrenched along the Piave River and the SPAD *squadriglie*, re-equipped and resettled in new aerodromes, remained eager to engage the enemy – literally with a vengeance.

THE COMBATANTS

AÉRONAUTIQUE MILITAIRE

The French SPAD VII was the product of a steady, rather logical process of fighter development that had begun with Lewis machine guns mounted above the wings of Nieuport 11s or wedge-shaped bullet deflectors on the propellers of Morane-Saulnier monoplanes, but which quickly gave way to synchronised weapons similar to the interrupter gear on the German Fokker Eindeckers. Although the Nieuport 17 and its progeny had a few diehard adherents, most notably Charles Nungesser, the majority of the French airmen who flew the SPAD were as sold on it as the revered and influential Georges Guynemer had been from the onset.

SPAD VII S239 of N102 undergoes maintenance in front of a typical Bessonneau hangar at Corbeaulieu aerodrome in March 1917. (SHAA B76.1857)

Pilots of N37, one of whom wears a fur coat in anticipation of cold conditions at altitude, check the ammunition belt before it is loaded into the magazine of the SPAD VII behind them. The interrupter gear that Hispano-Suiza engineer Marc Birkigt devised for the fighter's single 0.303-in Vickers machine gun proved chronically prone to jamming. (Greg VanWyngarden)

From late 1916 to late 1917, when twin-gun SPAD XIIIs began appearing in quantity, the only thing that delayed the VII's universal adoption was the rate at which SPAD and its licensed subcontractors could build them. Until there were enough to go around, many French units throughout 1917 and into early 1918 made do with their nimbler, but slower and more fragile Nieuports.

One of many examples can be seen in N124 'Lafayette'. Arriving on 6 November 1916, the unit's first SPADs went to its French commander, Capt Georges Thenault, and his deputy, Lt Alfred de Laage de Meux, but they were frequently flown by its American personnel, particularly the *escadrille's* paladin, Adj G. Raoul Lufbery. Writing about one mixed patrol, Sgt James R. McConnell (who preferred the Nieuport 17 until his death in one on 19 March 1917) described how 'de Laage in his swift SPAD races back and fourth in large detours, so as not to outdistance the rest of us. It gives you a feeling of confidence to see him manoeuvring above, for no finer soldier ever lived'.

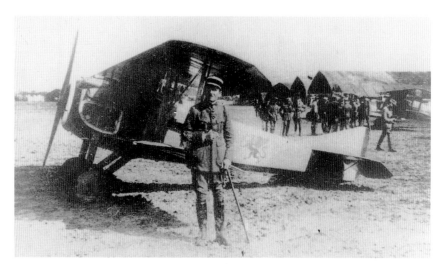

Typifying the expanding organisation of the French air service is Capt Edouard Duseigneur, leader of *Groupe de Combat* 11, whose SPAD VII displays the red griffon that served as his personal emblem on all his aeroplanes. His command, which he held from January 1917 through to June 1918, included *escadrilles* N12, N31, N48 and N57. (SHAA B76.1871)

Jacques Allez, shown beside
his SPAD VII while serving with
SPA65, was credited with two
probable victories with the
unit and then served on the
staff of *Groupe de Combat* 13
as a sous-lieutenant.
On 7 October 1918 he was
given command of newly
formed SPA173 and promoted
to lieutenant ten days later,
but the war ended before
the unit could enter combat.
(SHAA B83.1276)

French fighter pilot training evolved alongside their machines in an equally logical process. Initially, reconnaissance or bomber pilots who displayed extraordinary aggressiveness toward enemy aircraft they encountered were recommended for transfer to *chasse* units. Most, like René Fonck, René Dorme, Jean Chaput and André Martenot de Cordoux, had distinguished themselves in the slow but nimble Caudron G 4, although a similar performance in a lumbering Voisin 3 led to Charles Nungesser's transfer to N65.

As fighter units proliferated, the French training programme began earmarking pilots as they earned their brevets, either on clipped-wing Blériot 'roulleurs' or 'pingouins', followed by flyable Blériot XIs at Pau or on dual-control Caudron G 3s at Avord. 'After you took the test circuit', Martenot stated, 'the commandant, observing the steadiness and skill of the student, would choose the pilot for his role. The pilot was then trained further on more advanced aircraft – Nieuports for scout

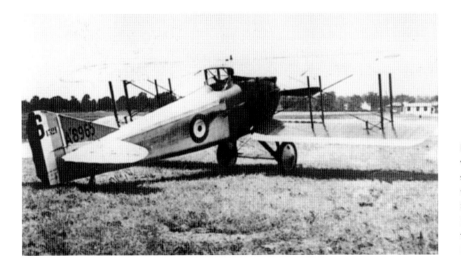

French-built SPAD VII S1321
wears RFC roundels and the
serial number A'8965. British
firms such as Mann, Egerton
& Co Ltd and L Blériot
(Aeronautics) also built
the type under licence.
(Jon Guttman)

ARMAND PINSARD

Born at Nercillac, Charente, on 28 May 1887, Armand Pinsard entered military service with the 2e *Régiment de Spahis* in Morocco in 1906, and was decorated twice by 27 June 1910. Transferring to aviation in May 1912 and earning military pilot's brevet No 210 on 3 September, MdL Pinsard was awarded the *Médaille Militaire* for his performance during the 1913 army manoeuvres.

When war broke out Adj Pinsard was assigned to *escadrille* MS23 and was promoted to sous-lieutenant in November 1914. On 8 February 1915, however, he was forced to land in enemy lines, where he and his observer, Sous-Lt Amaudrio de Chaffard, were taken prisoner. After several unsuccessful attempts, on 26 March Pinsard and Capt Victor Ménard escaped and returned to French territory on 10 April.

After rehabilitation and a promotion to lieutenant, Pinsard was assigned to N26, commanded by Ménard, on 8 July. There, he received SPAD VII S122 (allegedly the first example to see frontline service), which he used to score his first aerial victory on 7 September. That same day he was made a *Chevalier de la Légion d'Honneur*. Claiming his second success on 1 November, Pinsard left N26 on 12 December to take command of N78, with which unit he would down another 14 German aeroplanes before being injured in a flying accident on 12 June 1917.

Following a lengthy recovery, Pinsard returned to the front late in 1917 as commander of his first wartime squadron, now designated SPA23. There, he raised his score to 27 on 22 August 1918, and on the 30th he was made an *Officier de la Légion d'Honneur*. By war's end he had also received the *Croix de Guerre* with 19 palms and the British Military Cross.

Returning to the colours during World War II, Pinsard commanded *Groupement de Chasse* 21 until he was wounded in a bombing raid on 6 June 1940, resulting in the loss of a leg.

Following France's capitulation, however, he became Inspector General for the *Légion des Volontaires Française Contre le Bolchévisme*, which sent French volunteers to fight alongside the Germans on the Eastern Front. For this he was convicted of collaboration after the war and sentenced to life imprisonment, but was subsequently pardoned.

Armand Pinsard died at Ceyzeriat while attending a dinner being held by *Les Vielles Tiges* association on 10 May 1953.

---

pilots, Voisin pushers for bomber training, or the Caudron or Farman for reconnaissance training'.

Typically, *chasse* training would include specialised classes and practice in aerobatics at Pau and gunnery at Cazeaux. If he had not moved from Nieuports to SPADs by that time, the pilot got his chance while awaiting a unit assignment at the *Groupe Division d'Entrainement* (GDE) at Plessis-Belleville. Barring any accidents at that late state in the game, he would ultimately move on to a frontline *escadrille de chasse*, where his first few days were spent familiarising himself with the sector under the eyes of his commander and squadronmates, before being committed in deadly earnest.

WILLIAM J. C. KENNEDY-COCHRAN-PATRICK

Indisputably the highest-scoring SPAD ace in the RFC – and arguably its most successful exponent against the Albatros D III – was No. 23 Sqn's William John Charles Kennedy-Cochran-Patrick. Born in Ireland the son of Sir Noel Kennedy-Cochran-Patrick on 25 May 1896, he was educated at Cambridge University and served in the Rifle Brigade before joining the RFC.

After qualifying as a pilot in April 1915, Lt Kennedy-Cochran-Patrick proved such a skilful flyer that he was made a test pilot at No. 1 Aeroplane Depot at St Omer. There he probably would have stayed had a German two-seater not made a long-range flight over his area on 26 April 1916. Taking off in Nieuport 5172, Kennedy-Cochran-Patrick shot the intruder down near Hazebrouck, then landed to find the crew of Uffz Hans Hviires and Ltn Georg Jesko von Puttkammer of *Kampfgeschwader* 5 dead. That action earned Kennedy-Cochran-Patrick the Military Cross (MC) and a transfer to No. 70 Sqn, equipped with Sopwith 1½ Strutters. He scored victories on 14 and 15 September 1916 with this unit, although in both actions his observers, 2Lt E. W. Burke and Capt F. G. Glenday, were killed.

Promoted to captain, Kennedy-Cochran-Patrick was reassigned to No. 23 Sqn in 1917, where he reopened his account – and 'made ace' – by driving two Albatros D IIIs

down out of control (OOC) on 22 April. He was credited with a two-seater OOC on 26 April and ended the month with an Albatros D III in flames over Inchy en Barrois. Kennedy-Cochran-Patrick downed a D III OOC on 2 May, and was flying SPAD VII B1580, which would figure in all of his subsequent successes, when he destroyed another D III in flames west of Bourlon Wood on the 11th, killing Offstv Edmund Nathanael, a 15-victory ace of *Jasta* 5. Kennedy-Cochran-Patrick shared in bringing down two D IIIs on 13 May and destroyed another on the 20th. Four more aeroplanes fell to his guns in June, and he scored two more 'doubles' on 6 and 7 July. On 16 July, he destroyed an Albatros D V for his 21st, and final, victory, at which point he was promoted to major and given command of No. 60 Sqn. He had also been awarded a bar to his MC and later the Distinguished Service Order.

At the end of 1917 Kennedy-Cochran-Patrick returned to England to serve in the Training Division of the Air Board, then came around full circle when he was posted back to No. 1 Aeroplane Depot in 1918. Postwar, Kennedy-Cochran-Patrick did a lot of work undertaking aerial surveys, and while taking off from Baraghwanath Airport near Johannesburg, South Africa, on 27 September 1933, his de Havilland Dragon stalled at 250ft and crashed, killing both him and his passenger, Sir Michael Oppenheimer.

ROYAL FLYING CORPS

Coincident with the transition of No. 19 Sqn from BE 12s to SPAD VIIs in February 1917 came a new commander, Maj Hubert D. Harvey-Kelly. The first RFC pilot to arrive on French soil at the start of the war – in a BE 2a of No. 2 Sqn on 13 August 1914 – Harvey-Kelly was also credited with Britain's first air-to-air victory when he attacked a German Taube with his pistol on 25 August, compelling its crew to land and flee into the woods. He then landed beside the aircraft, set it alight on the ground and took off again.

After familiarisation flights at St Omer and gunnery training at Camiers, Harvey-Kelly moved his squadron to Vert Galant in March 1917. On 17 March, he reported:

At about 1030 hrs I was at 13,000ft when I saw a large two-seater and an Albatros scout about 4,000ft above him. I made for the two-seater and gave him a burst at long range and then climbed quickly and got above the scout. The scout turned east with its engine on and its nose down slightly. The SPAD, however, quickly caught him. Fire was opened about 200ft above him. A jam occurred after the first round and the engagement was broken off. The jam was cleared and the gun fired satisfactorily.

At about 1110 hrs I saw another Albatros scout above me. On manoeuvring for position, the SPAD easily outclimbed the Albatros, which then dived away. The SPAD followed and opened fire at about 150ft, and again the gun jammed after the first round. This jam could not be freed in the air and the machine returned on this account.

Harvey-Kelly's experience showed that the SPAD VII could hold its own against the best the Germans had, provided its Vickers gun did not jam – which, as all who flew the aeroplane found out, it was all too prone to do.

AVIAZIONE DEL REGIO ESERCITO

The development of the Italian fighter force was considerably influenced by France, both in terms of equipment and organisation. Its first fighter pilots were initially trained in French schools, and shortly before Italy's entry in the war on the Allied side Macchi obtained a licence to build Nieuport 10s, first as fighters and later as fighter trainers.

In January 1916 there were four *squadriglie da caccia* within the *Aviazione del Regio Esercito*, and they received their first single-seat Nieuport 11s in April. By December they had been redesignated as *70ª, 71ª, 72ª* and *73ª Squadriglie,* and been joined by four more units. Of those, the first four and *75ª* were organised within III *Gruppo* in emulation of the French *groupes de combat. 76ª* was slated to be the nucleus of

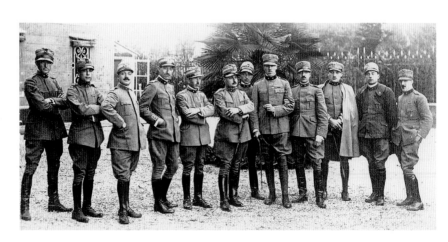

Members of Italy's elite SPAD VII equipped *91ª Squadriglia* include, fourth from left, Maggiore Pier Ruggiero Piccio (24 victories), eighth from left, Capt Francesco Baracca (34), and ninth from left, Capt Fulco Ruffo di Calabria (20). (Italian Embassy via Jon Guttman)

I *Gruppo*, with *77ª* performing a similar role for II *Gruppo*, while *74ª* remained an autonomous unit for the defence of Milan.

As more French aircraft arrived in 1917 (including the Hanriot HD 1, designed by the French firm to an Italian specification for licence production by Macchi) the *Aviazione del Regio Esercito* established its first aerial gunnery school. As of 20 November 1917, the fighter force had been organised around 14 *squadriglie* in six *gruppi*, plus the autonomous *73ª Squadriglia* in Thessaloniki, Macedonia, and *260ª* and *261ª Squadriglie*, defending Venice with Macchi M 5 flying boat fighters. By year-end *71ª* and *91ª Squadriglie* were fully or primarily equipped with SPAD VIIs.

As with their colleagues of other nations, Italian airmen were guided by professionalism and a sense of their rare status. Squadron esprit de corps depended upon a sense of 'family' that underlay the separation between commissioned and enlisted ranks, for which the leaders set the example.

Sottotenente Francesco Carlo Lombardi recalled his combat tour from August 1917 to August 1918 with *71ª Squadriglia* as 'one of the best years I have ever spent. Nos 77 and 80 together comprised the 13th Fighter Group, but I called it the 13th Fatigue Group because actual air fighting was very rare indeed. To indulge in it one had to steal flying hours from what free time was left after escorting reconnaissance aeroplanes, bombers and photographic machines, also ground-strafing and bombing the trenches with little five kilo bombs, all of which might add up to eight or nine hours daily. But we were all keen, cheerful and contented – a really happy atmosphere.

'Credit for this must go primarily to the group CO Capitano Mario Gordesco. I never once heard him give an order – he suggested, he proposed. "It might be a good thing to", or "would you mind", "could you" etc. So there was always more volunteers than a job required'.

77ª was equally well served by a succession of good squadron leaders, such as aces Capitano Pier Ruggiro Piccio, Tenente Ferruccio Ranza and, in March 1918, Tenente Alberto Marazzani, who was a steady, even-tempered 30-year-old known as 'il Vecio' ('the Old Man'). The squadron's youngest pilot, 20-year-old Lombardi, aka 'il Piccinin' ('the Kid' or 'Tich'), said 'I was always fond of him because he treated me like a scatter-brained younger brother'. An example of the familiarity and professionalism that coexisted within each Italian unit was exemplified by a junior NCO on *77ª Squadriglia*'s staff, as recounted by Lombardi:

The cowling panels of a SPAD VII delivered to the Italian air service are removed to show details of the engine and armament. (Greg VanWyngarden)

German *Jastas* were generally divided into two *Ketten* of four or five each, if they could muster full strength. Austro-Hungarian patrols varied more, from two to ten, depending on what was available. How much cooperation occurred when they made contact with the enemy was often determined by the leadership qualities of the flight or squadron commander. The British usually flew in V-shaped flights of three to seven aircraft in 1917, and would continue to do so until the Battle of Britain in 1940. French and Italian SPAD VIIs sometimes operated in twos, and experienced pilots with a sound operational rapport could provide one another with reasonably good mutual support, both offensively and defensively.

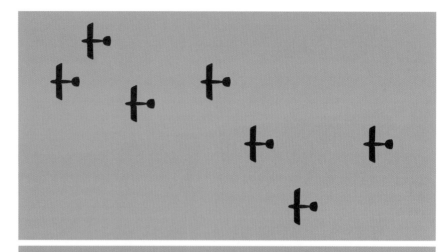

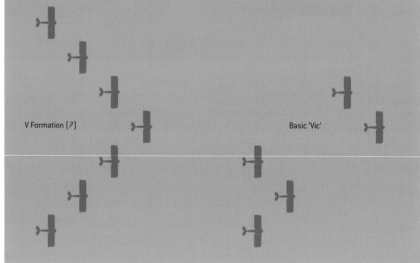

V Formation (?)

Basic 'Vic'

As the Adjutant's Orderly we had a dear delightful Territorial corporal from Calabria, who addressed everyone in the most informal terms, although he was highly conscientious and precise in the fulfilment of his duties. The moment an aeroplane landed he would go out and demand details of the flight – route followed, nature of mission, altitude, combats if any, number of rounds fired, etc., etc.

LUFTSTREITSKRÄFTE

The most notable aspect of German fighter activity throughout 1917 was its emphasis on defence, a stance that allowed pilots to make the most of the Albatros' strengths while avoiding exposure to its literal weaknesses. Germans often referred to British airmen as being more 'sporting' than the French, unaware that their aggressive OPs were dictated more by policy than knight-errantry. Similarly, a British pilot ignorant of the *Jastas'* tactical dicta might well have questioned German courage.

The average fighter pilot in the *Luftstreitskräfte* in early 1917 had already served in a reconnaissance or bombing unit before requesting a transfer, or being seconded due to displays of aggressiveness, to the fighter school established at Valenciennes. *Jagdstaffeln* usually maintained a clear separation between the enlisted ground personnel who lived on the aerodrome close to the hangars and aircraft, and the pilots – officers and enlisted – who found cosier accommodation in local buildings that often took the form of châteaux. After *Jasta* 2's grand success of 17 September 1916, however, Hptm Oswald Boelcke established a new tradition by opening the *Kasino* to all ranks for the evening's celebration.

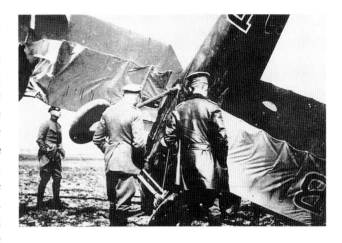

The day after Ltn Heinrich Kroll, a successful member of *Jasta* 9, was placed in command of *Jasta* 24 on 1 July 1917, he wrote home about how that unit's camaraderie had developed since the previous year:

All pilots, officers and NCOs live in the same mess. The place is so small that we must share rooms, but we all work, eat, sleep and play together. This is a good thing for morale. Should a member not fit into the group, it is an easy matter to remove him. This comradeship extends to air fighting as well. This morning one of our members was engaged in an air fight. We thought he would be the victor, so we placed ourselves in formation and flew defensively while our man brought down the enemy.

As soon as he was finished we started off again, and I saw two of my pilots fighting with the enemy. I charged in, with some others, not to bring down the enemy, but to protect our pilots. I led the enemy away since they then attacked me, believing themselves to have an easier victim. My pilots were then able to bring them both down. When we landed, the two pilots told me that both had

HEINRICH KROLL

Born in Flatzby, Flensberg, on 3 November 1894, Heinrich Claudius Kroll was the son of a schoolmaster. Indeed, he was taking examinations for a similar career when war broke out. Kroll volunteered for service with the local Fusilier Regiment Nr 86 'Queen Augusta Victoria' in Flensberg on 6 August 1914, but went to the front with Reserve Infantry Regiment Nr 92 instead. On 31 December he took part in the Battle of Hartmannswillerkopf and was subsequently awarded the Iron Cross Second Class, as well as being commissioned in May 1915.

Transferring to the air service in January 1916, Kroll trained at *Flieger Ersatz Abteilung* 3 at Gotha and in late April was sent to FA 17, with whom he flew Rumpler C Is over the Champagne sector. In October the unit received two Albatros scouts for escort, which Kroll flew until November, when he was assigned to fly fighters full time with *Jasta* 9.

In spite of an inauspicious debut when he was forced down in German lines by a Caudron of *escadrille* C222 on 24 November, Kroll was awarded the Iron Cross First Class on 12 February 1917. He came into his stride on 1 May with a 'SPAD VII' west of Moronvillers. Curiously, his victim was actually Nieuport 23 N2675, whose pilot, Sgt Georges Segond of N88, was killed.

Kroll claimed two SPADs on 7 May, one of which was flown by Adj Voilleau of N75, who was posted missing in action, and another on the 20th. His fifth victory, a SPAD over Fort de la Pompelle, turned out to be one of France's leading aces -- Sous-Lt René Dorme of N3, whose score stood at 23 when he was killed. After probably downing another SPAD on 30 May, Ltn Kroll was given command of Royal Saxon *Jasta* 24 on 1 July.

Now flying Albatros D V 2075/17, Kroll was credited with an SE 5 of No. 56 Sqn on 20 July, but on the 27th he was shot down in flames over Menin by a SPAD VII flown by American volunteer Capt Clive W. Warman of No. 23 Sqn RFC, although Kroll managed to survive unhurt. He resumed his scoring with a Sopwith Triplane on 12 August, and his tally steadily rose to 20 by 22 February 1918, when he received the Knight's Cross of the Hohenzollern House Order, and to 23 when he was awarded the *Orden Pour le Mérite* on 29 March. By then Kroll's command responsibilities extended to *Jagdgruppe* 12 (which consisted of his *Jasta* 24s, as well as 44 and 79b),

attached to the 18. *Armee* for the *Kaiserschlacht* offensive. Kroll and his men soldiered on as best they could with Albatros D Vs and Pfalz D IIIs until 25 May, when the first Fokker D VIIs arrived.

On 18 June, with 27 victories to his name, Kroll received the Knight's Cross Second Class with Swords of the Order of Albert. A SPAD on 30 June raised his tally to 30, but on 27 July he was again shot down in flames — and again emerged unscathed. Two victories on 8 August and another the next day brought his total to 33, but during a fight over Omencourt on 14 August he was hit in the left shoulder. Although Kroll duly landed intact, the severity of his wound put him out of the war.

An oberleutnant by the time the conflict ended, Kroll joined the Hamburg police and following the Kapp Putsch he recovered the body of fellow ace and *Freikorps* member Rudolf Berthold, killed in a street fight with communists on 15 March 1920. Taking a clerk's job in 1922, Kroll regained his pilot's licence and joined the Hamburg Flying Club in 1928, also becoming a commercial pilot for the LVG company in 1929. He died of pneumonia on 21 February 1930, however, and was buried in Ohlsdorf cemetery.

been victorious. Their joy was great! After landing, it was discovered that the spar in my wing had failed. This would have resulted in a certain crash had I flown again. Working together gives the commanding officer much support for this difficult job.

The French and the English fight completely differently. The Frenchman attacks only when he has superior numbers or when he has the tactical advantage, otherwise he tries to evade fighting and thinks only of his own safety. The English always attack and fight to the end. Some Englishmen do this without any tactics or plan. The enemy machines always outnumber us, and the SPAD and the Sopwith are very good aeroplanes. We have greater morale and enthusiasm than the enemy, and this ensures that we win.

KUK LUFTFAHRTRUPPEN

Austria-Hungary's first fighters in November 1915 were 13 German-supplied Fokker E Is and E IIIs, which were redesignated A Is and A IIIs for 'Abwehr', or defence. They and the indigenously produced Brandenburg D I or KD (*Kampf-Doppeldecker*), which began reaching the front late in 1916, were distributed in small detachments to escort two-seaters in the *Fliegerkompagnien*.

Soon after the Albatros D III (Oef) began reaching the front the KuK *Luftfahrtruppen*, or LFT, underwent a reorganisation. An order on 25 July called for more specialised, homogeneous units, categorised by a letter after their number. These included 'D' for *Division*, (reconnaissance, artillery spotting and ground troop support at divisional level); 'F' for *Fernaufklärungs* (long-range reconnaissance missions); 'G' for *Grossflugzeug* (six large bombers with four fighter escorts); 'S' for *Schlachtflieger* (ground attack); Rb for *Reihenbildung* (long-range photo-reconnaissance); 'P' for *Photoaufklärungs* (camera-equipped single-seat scouts for tactical frontline work); 'K' for *Korps* (support operations); and 'J' for *Jagd* (fighters).

Theoretically, each *Jagdfliegerkompagnie* had 18 fighters in three six-aeroplane *Kette*. Personnel included six pilot officers, a technical officer, an administrative officer (*Kanzleioffizier*) and 12 non-commissioned pilots, as well as 18 mechanics and 58 other ground support personnel. Those numbers would later increase on paper, some *Fliks* in

Bassano airfield, home to *Flik* 2/D in the summer of 1918, lies amid the alpine terrain that characterised the Italian front throughout the war, imposing its special constraints on the size of the front and the activities of the armies and air forces that fought there. A reconnaissance unit, *Flik* 2/D had its own fighters for escort and scouting duties, of which Albatros D III (Oef) 153.95 can be seen in the background. (Greg VanWyngarden)

Hptm Godwin Brumowski (left) and Oblt Frank Linke-Crawford chat in front of Brumowski's red, skull-marked Albatros D III (Oef) 153.45 and Linke-Crawford's falcon-marked 153.16 at *Flik* 41/J's airfield at Torresella in December 1917. (Greg VanWyngarden)

the Sixth Army having as many as 20 aeroplanes in February-March 1918. In practice, however, pilots and available aircraft generally varied from four to ten per *Flik*.

Most Austro-Hungarian aces scored their first victories – and in many cases most of them – in two-seaters, particularly the outstanding Brandenburg C I. Typically, Hptm Godwin Brumowski had downed his fifth opponent in a C I shortly before being given command of newly formed *Flik* 41/J. First, however, he was sent to acquaint himself with the latest developments in aerial combat over the Western Front, flying with *Jasta* 24 from 19 to 27 March 1917 and meeting Manfred von Richthofen. Brumowski was profoundly influenced by the experience. After returning to Italy in April he took steps to turn *Flik* 41/J into an elite unit like von Richthofen's *Jasta* 11. He even painted some of his own aeroplanes red, with the addition of skulls on the fuselage.

In June Brumowski – displaying an outspokenness worthy of von Richthofen – reported to his superiors that 'the KD is absolutely useless, and the best pilots (and only they can fly the type) are shackled, their nerves shattered. Many have perished in crashes on the airfield before their expert skill allowed them to achieve anything in battle'. In July 1917 Oeffag D IIIs began to reach *Flik* 41/J. On 21 August, when the 11th Battle of the Izonso began, Brumowski's unit had seven D IIIs and three D Is.

Like the Austro-Hungarian army, the LFT retained a stricter divide between officers and enlisted men than its German counterpart. How strict varied with each commander. Among the most hide-bound was Oblt d R Ernst Strohschneider, who led *Fliks* 42/J and 61/J. 'The separation of officers and non-officers was a disruptive thing', remarked second-ranking LFT ace Julius Arigi in a 1977 interview with historian Marty O'Connor. 'Many officers managed to avoid this and treated the NCOs well. Of all the officers I flew with, Strohschneider was the worst to the non-officers'.

Also varying with the commander was the degree that ethnicity mattered in the LFT. Ltn Joszef von Meier, for example, seemed to favour fellow Hungarians in *Flik* 55/J, even an NCO such as Offstv Joszef Kiss, who hailed from his home city of Poszony (called Pressburg by the Austrians, but now the Slovakian capital of Bratislava). The Sudeten German-born Strohschneider, in contrast, regarded one's commission more important than one's nationality. While commanding *Flik* 42/J he shared seven of his 15 victories, and was fast friends with Hungarian Ltn d R Ferenc Gräser. However, one of *Flik* 42/J's Hungarian NCOs, Offstv Frigyes Hefty, noted in his memoirs that when he received the Gold Medal for Bravery in October 1917, Strohschneider was the only officer in the unit who did not congratulate him.

COMBAT

BLOODY APRIL

The first known encounter between an Albatros D III and an RFC SPAD VII occurred on 19 March 1917 when No. 19 Sqn's 2Lt S. S. B. Purves went missing from a morning patrol. Last seen at 0900 hrs, he was evidently brought down at Homblières, east of St Quentin, at 1010 hrs German time by *Jasta* 5's Ltn Kurt Schneider in D III 2244/16. SPAD A6633 was captured intact, but its pilot did not remain a PoW long before managing to escape.

Brought down intact by Ltn Kurt Schneider of *Jasta* 5, SPAD VII A6633 was No. 19 Sqn's –and the RFC's – first known loss to an Albatros D III, on 19 March 1917. The pilot, 2Lt S. S. B. Purves, was taken prisoner, but later managed to escape. (Greg VanWyngarden)

The first week of April 1917 saw the Germans falling back on St Quentin and the Hindenburg Line. Ltn d R Hans Auer of *Jasta* 26 claimed a 'Nieuport' over Sennheim on the 5th, but the only French loss was Cpl Jacques Herubel of N78, killed in action near Jonchère in a SPAD VII.

On 6 April, while the United States was declaring war on Germany, Canadian Capt Kenneth M. McCallum of No. 23 Sqn was credited with a German two-seater. In return the Germans claimed two French SPADs, Ltn Hartmuth Baldamus of *Jasta* 9 downing one northwest of Fresnes and Ltn Heinrich Bongartz of *Jasta* 36 getting the other one at Vitry-les-Reims. The former's victim, Lt Auguste Lorillard of N48, was killed while attacking a German kite balloon. Lt Jean Mistarlet of N31 succeeded in burning a balloon at Lavannes before Bongartz brought him down in SPAD S244. Mistarlet survived as a PoW.

The next day, *Groupe de Combat* 13, consisting of *escadrilles* N15, N65, N88 and N124, moved to Ham to support the British assault on Arras. N124's American volunteers completed their move on the 8th, and at 1330 hrs that afternoon their French deputy commander, Lt de Laage de Meux, shot down Albatros D III 2234/16 north of St Quentin. The British found the pilot, Ltn Roland Nauck of *Jasta* 6, dead when they recovered the wreckage. The aircraft bore the serial G 21.

The Germans claimed four SPADs on 11 April, including 2Lt S. Roche of No. 23 Sqn, brought down and captured near Cuvillers at 0900 hrs by Ltn Hermann Frommherz of *Jasta* 'Boelcke'. Another was credited to Ltn Otto Bernert at 1230 hrs, but his opponent, Lt F. C. Troup, force-landed in British lines unharmed. At 1145 hrs two SPADs from N73 came to grief near Berry-au-Bac at the hands of Oblt Rudolf Berthold and Offstv Otto Hüttner of *Jasta* 14, Adj Albert Barioz being killed and a wounded Sgt Marcel Paris making it back to French lines.

No. 19 Sqn finally claimed its first Albatros D III on 13 April when Lt G. S. Buck drove one down OOC over Brebières. The Germans recorded no casualties that day, but they credited Ltn Albert Dossenbach of *Jasta* 36 with a French SPAD near Sapigneul. His victim was Sous-Lt Marcel Nogues of N12, then with two victories to his name. Five weeks later Nogues escaped and returned to action, raising his score to 13.

Newly arrived SPAD VIIs at N124 await application of the *escadrille's* Indian head marking at Ham aerodrome, where its American personnel had flown the 'Stars & Stripes' since 6 April 1917, when their country declared war on Germany. The unit's first SPAD VII victory over an Albatros D III was scored on 8 April by its French second-in-command, Lt Alfred de Laage de Meux. (Jon Guttman)

On 14 April No. 19 Sqn had its first run-in with *Jasta* 11 since von Richthofen's unit had fully re-equipped with strengthened Albatros D IIIs on the 5th. It did not go well for the British. While 'A' flight was on an OP along the Bailleul-Vitry-Sains-Bullecourt line it was jumped by the Germans. Ltn Kurt Wolff reported that his opponent almost got him before he managed to turn the tables and shoot his assailant down west of Bailleul, killing Lt Edward W. Capper. The other SPAD, credited as being driven down south of Vimy by the 'Red Baron's' brother, Ltn Lothar von Richthofen, was flown by Lt J. W. Baker, who was wounded but managed to get back to Le Hameau before crash-landing. In the French sector, Ltn Josef Veltjens of *Jasta* 14 claimed a SPAD near Craonne for his first victory, but the French recorded no losses. They would not be so lucky the following day.

After taking off at 0520 hrs on the 15th, MdL Achille Louis Papeil of N3 tried to attack an Albatros over Prouvais, only to come under fire from another. Papeil dived with both Germans after him, but suddenly pulled up and over his original quarry, Vzfw Georg Strasser of *Jasta* 17.

Rittm Manfred *Freiherr* von Richthofen, commander of *Jasta* 11, suits up beside his Albatros D III at Roucourt aerodrome in April 1917. That month saw the 'Red Baron', his Albatros and his *Staffel* at the top of their game, much to the detriment of the RFC. (Greg VanWyngarden)

Strasser's *Staffel* mate, Vzfw Julius Buckler, who had already attacked the SPAD, now came at it again. Buckler's guns had jammed, but as he closed on his opponent Papeil sideslipped down, flipped his aeroplane over in the process of landing and was taken prisoner. Buckler later recorded his impressions of the 'nice young fellow, a sergeant, and a real Frenchman', while misspelling his name:

Why had Papaine landed? A grazing wound on his left cheek alone could not be the cause of it, but now it was revealed that he had in fact been the victim of a jammed machine gun, and that during the fight we had both been bluffing the same way. However, I had the better nerves. Besides that, I had put two bullets through his fuel tank, and that was the compelling reason for his landing.

Buckler also thought he had heard Papeil refer to his lost SPAD 'with great love and passion as *ma Lola*', which he and his squadronmates, liking the sound of it, corrupted into 'Malaula'. 'It became a signal, a battle cry', he wrote, 'The battle cry of our *Staffel!*'

Papeil, like Purves and Nogues, later escaped and was an instructor at the GDE when the war ended.

Another French loss on 15 April was Cpl Emile Quaissard of N102, shot down over Nauroy by Ltn Werner Albert of *Jasta* 31, but the worst debacle befell N15. It began

at 1030 hrs when Lt Paul Bergeron led a raid against *Jasta* 21's aerodrome at St Mard, only to be attacked and brought down near Sery by Uffz Max Zachmann of *Jasta* 21. Bergeron's scattered flight was then set upon by *Jasta* 36, Ltn Dossenbach bringing Adj Denis Epitalon down between St Fergeux and Rethel, and Vzfw Hans Mitzkeit likewise downing Sgt Nicholas Bouisson near Thrugny. All three N15 pilots became PoWs.

On 16 April Nivelle finally launched his delayed offensive, which became known as the Second Battle of the Aisne. French airmen claimed three enemy aeroplanes and two balloons that day, to which Brig Rigault of N73 contributed a D III and a balloon. The former, downed north of Cormicy, was probably Vzfw Rieger of *Jasta* 17, who crashed with his controls shot away at Pontavert, eight kilometres northwest of Cormicy, surviving with severe injuries.

Sous-Lt René Dorme of N3 took on six Albatros D IIIs west of Orainville on 19 April and destroyed one northeast of Brimont for his 19th victory, probably killing Ltn Paul Herrmann of *Jasta* 31. N69 suffered the temporary loss of Lt Hervé Conneau, wounded by Ltn Werner Marwitz of *Jasta* 9 southwest of Auberive.

No. 23 Sqn's 2Lt R. L. Keller claimed an Albatros OOC over Cagnicourt on 21 April. The only German loss to SPADs that day, however, was Ltn Günther von der Hyde of *Jasta* 9, killed over Nauroy at 2000 hrs – one of two aircraft downed between Nauroy and Moronvilliers that were credited to Lt Pinsard of N78.

The weather on Sunday, 22 April, was described as fine but cloudy. That evening a flight of No. 23 Sqn machines, together with Sopwith Pups of 3 Naval Squadron, was escorting FE 2bs of No. 18 Sqn when the SPADs became separated from the others. The 'Fees' dropped their bombs and the four German fighters that turned up were driven off by the Pups.

Meanwhile, at 1900 hrs, No. 23 Sqn's pilots spotted what they thought to be a British formation between Marcoing and Havrincourt Wood. As they climbed to join it, however, they came under attack by what turned out to be Albatros D IIIs of *Jastas* 5 and 12. Using their height advantage, *Jasta* 12's CO, Hptm Paul Henning von Osterroht, drove down a SPAD south of Marcoing at 2005 hrs, while *Jasta* 5's Offstv Edmund Nathanael claimed a second one at Ribécourt-la-Tour. 2Lts K. R. Furniss (A6695) and F. C. Craig (A6682) were captured, Furniss dying of his wounds. At 2010 hrs Vzfw Reinhold Jörke of *Jasta* 12 was credited with a SPAD downed in Allied lines, its pilot, Capt Ken McCallum, being wounded in action. Vzfw Ernst Dahlmann claimed a SPAD over *Jasta* 5's old aerodrome at Gonnelieu, but it was disallowed. *Jasta* 12's Ltn d R Friedrich Roth was credited with an aeroplane over Marcoing, but No. 23 Sqn suffered no other casualties. As it was, it had suffered plenty.

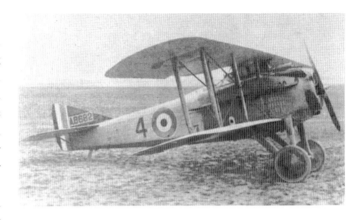

SPAD VII A6682, flown by 2Lt F. C. Craig of No. 23 Sqn, was photographed by the Germans after Hptm Paul Hennig von Osterroht of *Jasta* 12 brought it down on 22 April 1917. (Jon Guttman)

Although the Germans lost no men in the melee, 2Lt Keller claimed an Albatros OOC east of Cambrai, while Capt William J. C. Kennedy-Cochran-Patrick claimed two over Fontaine Notre Dame and Flequières. Coincidentally, both Nathanael's and Kennedy-Cochran-Patrick's successes brought their scores up to five. Their flightpaths were destined to cross again, with a different outcome – on 11 May Kennedy-Cochran-Patrick claimed a D III in flames west of Bourlon Wood at 1905 hrs, killing Nathanael.

On St George's Day, 23 April, No. 19 Sqn's CO, Maj Harvey-Kelly, bounced an Albatros over Graincourt at 1910 hrs and after firing 50-60 rounds at a range of 50 yards, reported that it crash-landed about a mile from Cambrai.

A D III was claimed OOC by 2Lt H. R. Stocken of No. 23 Sqn on 24 April, but the principal honours that day went to the French as Vzfw Rudolf Rath of *Jasta* 35 crashed to his death at Hagenbach in D III 2120/16, matching a claim by Adj Edmund Pillon of N82 for a fighter downed near Dannemarie. At 1720 hrs Cpl Marcel Henriot of N65 claimed a scout over the Fôret de Pinon for his first victory. His likely victim, Vzfw Max Wackwitz of *Jasta* 24, force landed at Bignicourt short of his aerodrome, but unhurt.

During a major outbreak of dogfighting on 26 April, at 1840 hrs No. 23 Sqn's Capt Ken McCallum was credited with two D IIIs OOC over Cambrai, while 2Lts Keller and G. C. Stead claimed two more OOC between Fontaine and Notre Dame.

Two of three SPAD VIIs of No. 23 Sqn brought down on 7 June 1917 brood forlornly in *Jasta* 10's hangars. B'1524 (foreground), in which Capt W. J. C. Kennedy-Cochran-Patrick had scored three of his 21 victories and 2Lt Douglas U. McGregor had used it to share in the destruction of an Albatros D III on 13 May, was brought down near Menin by Offstv Paul Aue and its wounded pilot, 2Lt F. W. Illingworth, captured. B'3460 was downed near Rumbeke by Uffz Hermann Brettel, its pilot, 2Lt Count L. T. B. de Balme also becoming a PoW. In addition, 2Lt George C. Stead in B1527 was driven down and captured at Comines by Offstv Max Müller of *Jasta* 28. (Bruno J. Schmäling via Jon Guttman)

The RFC's only SPAD casualty was B1537 flown by Lt James M. Child of No.19 Sqn, the aircraft having been attacked by five overzealous Sopwith Triplane pilots of 8 Naval Squadron. They mistook Child's SPAD for a German scout and put holes through its tailplane, fuselage and wings before the pilot managed to spin away with his engine full-on and force-land at Bellevue at 1900 hrs, fortunately unharmed. Lt Holmes came under attack from the same Triplanes but also managed to escape with a whole skin. Child would score again in his repaired B1537 the following day, but the incident led No. 19 Sqn to replace its black dumbbell fuselage marking with prominent blue, white and red fuselage bands, along with cockades on the wheel hubs.

SPAD VII A6753 of No. 19 Sqn displays a rotating set of radiator blinds to adjust engine cooling. The aeroplane was downed on 29 April 1917 by Ltn Lothar von Richthofen of Jasta 11 and Lt William N. Hamilton captured. (Greg VanWyngarden)

The French lost two SPADs on the 26th. Cpl Marcel Egret of N78 fell to Ltn Albert of *Jasta* 31, and at 1600 hrs Capt René Doumer, CO of N76 and a seven-victory ace, was killed north of Brimont in S1447 by Oblt Erich Hahn, CO of *Jasta* 19. The Germans also lost a leader at 1930 hrs, however, when three SPADs killed Oblt Max Reinhold, CO of *Jasta* 15, near Lierval. He was probably the unconfirmed 'scout' claimed between Réservoir and Trucy, about three kilometres from Lierval, by Sous-Lt Roland Baudoin of N80.

No further clashes between SPAD and Albatros took place until 29 April. That day No. 19 Sqn had sent two flights out when Wing Headquarters called for a third patrol. Maj Harvey-Kelly responded by personally leading Lt William N. Hamilton and 2Lt Richard Applin toward Douai. On the way they encountered three red-coloured and five silvery-grey D IIIs. Harvey-Kelly also noticed six Triplanes of 1 Naval Squadron nearby and, assuming that they would join in, he attacked the three red machines. The Triplanes did indeed engage five of the Germans in a 20-minute scrap, claiming three OOC, but it did Harvey-Kelly's men no good for the red trio

Disasters came as often by accident as from combat for both sides. On 29 April Capt Emile Billon du Plan, commander of N65, was killed when his SPAD VII S1452 crashed at Bonne-Maison. (SHAA B83.1280)

with whom they squared off were from *Jasta* 11, with Rittm Manfred von Richthofen at their head. The 'Red Baron's' account of the fight would have flattered No. 19 Sqn's men a bit, since he referred to the SPADs as a 'special squadron' organised to counter his *Staffel*:

Our aggressors thought themselves very superior to us because of the excellence of their apparatus. Immediately at the beginning of the encounter the aggressive became a defensive. Our superiority became clear. I tackled my opponent and could see how my brother and Wolff handled each their own enemy. The usual waltzing began. We were circling around one another. A favourable wind came to our aid. It drove us fighting away from the Front in the direction of Germany.

Von Richthofen got on the tail of Applin, who with 75 flying hours' total was the least experienced of the SPAD pilots:

I suppose I had smashed up his engine. At any rate, he made up his mind to land. I no longer give pardon to anyone. Therefore, I attacked him a second time and the consequence was that his whole machine went to pieces. His planes dropped off like pieces of paper and the body of the machine fell like a stone, burning fiercely. It dropped into a morass. It was impossible to dig it out, and I have never discovered the name of my opponent. He had disappeared. Only the end of the tail was visible, and it marked the place where he had dug his own grave.

Simultaneously with me, Wolff and my brother had attacked their opponents and had forced them to land not far from my victim.

We were very happy and flew home, hoping that the anti-Richthofen Squadron would often return to the fray.

Applin, who died near Lecluse, was the first of four victories von Richthofen would score that day, bringing his total to 52. Struck in the head by Wolff, Harvey-Kelly came down at Sailly-en-Ostrevent and died of his wounds in a German hospital three days later. More fortunate was Hamilton, driven down at Izel by Lothar von Richthofen and captured.

Devastating though Harvey-Kelly's loss was to No. 19 Sqn, no less so to *Jasta* 29 was the loss of its leader, Ltn Ludwig Dornheim, at Beine – probably to Lt Jean Béraud-Villars of N102, who claimed an enemy aircraft in flames northeast of Nauroy. Sous-Lt Georges Lebeau of N12 also claimed a scout over Orainville at 1745 hrs, probably wounding Ltn Peckmann of *Jasta* 15.

For all they had suffered in April, the SPADs had the last word on the 30th. Capt Kennedy-Cochran-Patrick claimed a D III in flames, possibly wounding Ltn Friedrich Mallinkrodt, a six-victory ace of *Jasta* 20, and 2Lt Standish Conn O'Grady claimed one OOC over Inchy-en-Artois. In the Aisne sector, Ltns Friedrich von Hartmann and Hermann Pfeiffer of *Jasta* 9 were both credited with SPADs, but the French lost none that day, whereas Ltn Werner Marwitz of *Jasta* 9 was killed over Nauroy, probably the enemy aircraft in flames north of Moronvillers credited to N81's CO, Lt Raymond Bailly.

FEROCITY OVER THE FRENCH SECTOR

The French had moved some of their most seasoned *groupes de combat* into the Chemin des Dames sector to support Nivelle's offensive, including the famed GC 11 *'Les Cigognes'* (*escadrilles* N3, N26, N73 and N103). Although more discrete than the British in how deep into German lines they flew unless the mission required it, their SPAD pilots took on their adversaries with a well-established élan.

First blood went to the Germans on 2 May when Cpl Paul Victor Oudard of N85 was taken prisoner in SPAD VII S1075. The only matching claim – probably misidentified – was a 'Nieuport 17' credited as brought down south of Beine by Ltn Wolfgang Güttler of *Jasta* 24. Vzfw Buckler of *Jasta* 17 forced a SPAD to land near Pontavert on 6 May. This was probably Lt Gaëtan de La Brunetière of N69, who was wounded but rejoined his unit. There could be no disputing the 'scout' credited to Lt René Pollet of N102 over Suippe on 15 May – *Jasta* 29 logged the death of Ltn Karl Pockrantz in a mid-air collision. Pollet's first victory, however, cost him his SPAD VII, S1199, and his life.

Early in the morning of 19 May No. 19 Sqn became embroiled in an impressive imbroglio near Arras, which also involved Triplanes of 'Naval 1'. Nearby, Lt A. R. Boeree and 21-year-old Capt William Jameson Cairnes attacked two two-seaters and the six red Albatros that accompanied them. When the fight degenerated into a wild melee of 'every man for himself', the Germans disengaged, but not before Cairnes had claimed a two-seater and a D III, his first two of an eventual six victories. On the debit side for No. 19 Sqn, 2Lt S. F. Allabarton was forced down with engine trouble and captured.

On the 23rd Cairnes forced down a red Albatros north of Brebières at 1730 hrs that was not credited, but at 1915 hrs squadronmate Lt Augustus H. Orlebar in SPAD A6663 claimed a D III in flames east of Douai. Orlebar's first of seven victories may have been Ltn Ernst *Ritter und Edler* von Lössl of *Jasta* 18, who succumbed to his injuries the next day.

Vengeance-driven Sous-Lt René Dorme of N3, at right, beside his 180hp SPAD VII S392, of which he said, 'My pressurised aircraft, which is tuned well, gives me absolute confidence'. He scored six confirmed victories in it, boosting his tally to 23, before being killed in action by Ltn Heinrich Kroll of *Jasta* 9 on 25 May 1917. (Louis Risacher album via Jon Guttman)

No. 19 Sqn had mixed fortunes on 25 May. Child downed a D III OOC west of Douai at 0645 hrs, but Lt H. G. P. Okeden and 2Lt E. A. Mearns were wounded, the former possibly being credited to Uffz Friedrich Gille of *Jasta* 12. Mearns later described how he had escaped an enemy fighter attacking him from below by executing a climbing vertical spiral, only to run into the fire of a nearby German two-seater's observer.

French fighters claimed ten victories on 25 May, including four by Capt Guynemer, but his *escadrille*, N3, lost its second-ranking ace. Sous-Lt René Dorme was about to visit a wounded friend, Adj Joseph Guiguet, when N73's commander, Lt Deullin, invited him on a last sortie for the day. The two aces departed Bonne-Maison at 1840 hrs. Deullin subsequently returned alone to report encountering four to six enemy fighters east of Reims, one of which he thought he saw Dorme shoot down before they became separated. After battling several Germans, Deullin eluded his pursuers, then returned to the scene of the fight and noticed a SPAD burning on the ground.

The most plausible of three enemy claims in the area that day came from *Jasta* 9, which reported a violent encounter near Fort de la Pompelle in which Ltn Otto von Breiten-Landenberg claimed a SPAD near Nauroy at 2005 hrs (1905 Allied time) and Ltn Heinrich Kroll downed another near Beine at 2015 hrs. The Germans recovered a watch from the wreckage of Kroll's victim, bearing the inscription, *'offert par la Maison L I P of Besanon to M. René Dorme'*.

Writing to his parents of the event on 11 June, Kroll stated, 'It was during a harsh swirling fight engaged at 5,300 metres and ended at less than 800 metres from the ground. He suddenly dived away and crashed with a burst of fire'. Breiten-Landenberg's victory, though also confirmed, may have been a case of double claiming or, just as likely, mistaking Deullin's evasive actions for he too being shot down.

On 26 May Ltn Otto Kissenberth of *Jasta* 16 destroyed a SPAD, killing Sous-Lt Cabaud of N37, but otherwise the Germans fared poorly. That day Ltn Udet of *Jasta* 15 was leading Ltns Hellmuth and Hewarth Wendel, Ltn d R Eberhard Hänisch and Offstv Willy Glinkermann on patrol in a V-shaped formation at an altitude of 2,000 metres amid a clear sky. Over Chermizy, a 'sixth sense' compelled Udet to make a half turn and look back – to see 'Puz' Hänisch's Albatros 'enveloped in fire and smoke'.

'Then his machine breaks up', Udet wrote. 'The fuselage dives straight down like a fiery meteor, the broken wing planes trundling after it. I am stunned as I stare over the side after the wreckage. An aircraft moves into the range of my sight and tears westward about 500 metres below me. The cockades blink up at me like malicious eyes. At the same time I have the feeling that it can only be Guynemer!

'I push down. I have to get him! But the wings of the Albatros are not up to the strain. They begin to flutter more and more, so that I fear the machine will disintegrate in the air. I give up the pursuit and return home.'

Contrary to Udet's supposition, Guynemer was credited with a two-seater that day. Hänisch was more likely an unconfirmed victory claimed by Sous-Lt Louis Milliat of N80 between Neuville and Chermizy.

Also killed was Uffz Erich Leyh of *Jasta* 29 over Caurel, matching a scout in flames credited to MdL Pierre de Cazenove de Pradines of N81. 'It was not until 26 May

OVERLEAF
Although the SPAD VII flew its first combat mission in August 1916 and Albatros D IIIs began reaching frontline units four months later, both were still in service at the time of the armistice in November 1918. Even at that late date French *escadrilles de chasse* generally consisted of 12 SPAD XIIIs, the spur reduction gear of whose Hispano-Suiza 8B engines were still prone to problems, and a 'backup' contingent of six direct-drive SPAD VIIs. SPA161's MdL Emile Vieil (one of the unit's original members from its formation on 5 January 1918) was flying a dawn patrol in one such SPAD VII when he went missing in action on 16 July 1918. His was apparently the SPAD credited as downed near Tahure at 0545 hrs by Ltn Franz Ray, commander of *Jasta* 49, an *Amerika Programm* unit that still had yet to receive Fokker D VIIs at that late stage of the war. Forced to settle for whatever was available, Ray preferred the OAW-built D III over the Albatros D V, D Va or any other fighter type short of the D VII Germany had to offer. This, Ray's 16th of 17 victories, may well have been the last encounter between these old, yet not quite outdated, adversaries.

1917 that I gained my first success in the air', he stated in a 1979 interview, 'and that turned out to be almost too quick and easy to be true. I was flying over Reims when I spotted another SPAD with an Albatros D V [sic] on its tail. I quickly turned, closed, fired and down went the Albatros, smoking'. It was Cazenove's first of seven victories.

On 29 May Udet lost another friend as Willy Glinkermann fell over Orgeval, matching a 'scout in flames' near Montchâlons credited to Sous-Lt Robert de Bruce of N75, but N3 lost Cpl Lucien Perot, the victim of Vzfw Hans Bowski of *Jasta* 14. The latter unit struck again on 1 June when Ltn Veltjens brought down Sgt Charles Durand of N75, who died of wounds soon after.

The heavy French losses during the Second Battle of the Aisne, climaxed by Dorme's death, reflected less on the SPAD VII than on the tactics employed by its pilots. Strategically, their constant patrolling over the frontlines was dictated by the commander of fighter units in the sector, Commandant Paul Fernand du Peuty, who called for 'the destruction of Boche aviation. Not a single fighter of their *groupes de combat* must be encountered within French lines. The time has come to give the best of our efforts, without paying attention to fatigue or losses'.

French tactical doctrine, however, was highly influenced by Capt Deullin, who wrote:

Fighting in groups is still in an embryonic stage. Using that tactic is interesting for ensuring mastery of a given point at a given time, but not to shoot down Boches. Up to now a group of only two has given good results.

In the wake of the losses he witnessed at the hands of German *Jasta*s deployed en masse – most personally that of Dorme – Deullin revised his opinion in a subsequent report:

Since the Somme offensive, which is to say about a year, conditions for the fighter force have completely changed. The enemy, trained by experience, has coordinated his efforts and formed perfectly disciplined two-seater patrols and single-seater patrols. Their cohesion has allowed them, first, to resist isolated attacks and then, in turn, to take the offensive and to quite easily shoot down the French who venture into the other side of the lines. After a few fruitless or even painful attempts, our fighters had to realise that the era of individualism was finished and they would have to seek another way.

RIVALRY RESUMED – OVER ITALY

Encounters between Italian SPAD VIIs and Austro-Hungarian Oeffag-Albatros D IIIs began occurring during the 11th Battle of the Isonzo in the late summer of 1917, but they were few and incidental compared to both fighter types' engagements with one another's two-seaters. On 17 September Tenente Giovanni Sabelli attacked a Brandenburg C I protected by an Albatros D III, and although a jammed gun forced him to disengage, the two-seater force landed in Austro-Hungarian lines and was credited to him. Sabelli, however, was himself jointly credited as shot down to the wounded Brandenburg crewmen, Zugsf Rudolf Planecky and Oblt Ernst von Szalay of *Flik* 34/D, and their escort, Fw Radames Iskra of *Flik* 41/J.

A more direct confrontation occurred at Caporetto, where the Italians faced specialised *Jagdfliegerkompagnien* combined with aggressively flown Albatros D IIIs and D Vs of *Jastas* 1, 31 and 39. There, the SPAD pilots of *77ᵃ* and *91ᵃ Squadriglie* gave as good as they got – to Austro-Hungarians and Germans alike.

Capt Francesco Baracca flew a new SPAD XIII on 22 October when he shot down two enemy two-seaters that turned out to be from FA 14 – the first Italian victories over German aircraft. Overcast skies limited aerial activity when the Central Powers struck at Caporetto on the 24th, routing the Italian army and taking 275,000 prisoners. The aerial struggle, resuming in earnest the next day, was a different story, as Baracca recalled:

> On the 25th, there was great activity. I had five fights with the Germans. At 1100 hrs I shot down an Austrian Albatros over San Marco (Gorizia) with Tenente Colonello Piccio. In the evening, I had my SPAD shot up and its longeron broken into pieces by enemy machine gun fire in an aerial dogfight.
>
> Two of my pilots fell during the fighting – Sabelli, downed in flames, and Ten Ferreri, shot down by enemy fighters over Tolmino during a battle between one of my patrols and enemy fighters. Ruffo shot down two enemies in flames, Piccio another one in flames over Cividale. We claimed six aeroplanes in all.

Baracca's and Piccio's first victim was a Brandenburg C I from *Flik* 19, whose crew was killed. In addition to the two victories that Baracca witnessed, Capts Fulco Ruffo di Calabria and Bartolomeo Constantini shared in a third. Capt Ferrucchio Ranza downed a DFC C V of FA 39 over Lom. Sabelli and Piccio tried to attack a two-seater when enemy fighters intervened, at which point Piccio suffered a gun jam and had to disengage. He was probably credited, along with the slain Sabelli, to Ltn Herbert Schröder and Vzfw Münnichow of German *Jasta* 1. Tenente Enrico Ferreri may have been the eighth of an eventual 28 victories for Oblt Benno Fiala *Ritter* von Fernbrugg, then in *Flik* 12/D and flying a Brandenburg D I.

While what remained of the Italian army fell back across the Tagliamento River, the relentless pace of aerial combat left *91ᵃ Squadriglia's* SPADs so worn out that its pilots had to fly Nieuport 17s and Hanriot HD 1s until the first week of November, when the unit completed its withdrawal from Pordenone to Padova aerodrome and new SPADs arrived.

Albatros D III (Oef)s of *Flik* 42/J at Prosecco in September 1917 include, from left, 153.58 flown by Stabsfeldwebel Frigyes Hefty and 153.42 flown by Zugsführer Nandor Udvardy. On 23 September Udvardy and Oblt d R Ernst Strohschneider were jointly credited with a SPAD VII 'in flames' over Novi Vas, probably flown by Capitano Francesco Baracca of *91ᵃ Squadriglia* – who in fact escaped unharmed for the second time in eight days. (Greg VanWyngarden)

Sottotenente Francesco Carlo Lombardi of *77ª Squadriglia* stands before his SPAD VII fitted with a cold-weather radiator cowling and adorned with the unit's red heart insignia behind the fuselage roundel. *'Il Piccinin'* Lombardi's victories included at least one German Albatros. (Roberto Gentilli)

On 4 November Sottotenente Francesco Lombardi of *77ª Squadriglia* was escorting a Caproni when he engaged a German fighter, which the bomber crew credited him with shooting down over Cividale. Such a claim deep in enemy-held territory would be forgivably dubious had not *Jasta* 39 indeed recorded the death of Flg Anton Huchler at Cividale. Two days later, during a morning patrol, Baracca and Parvis encountered a pair of Albatros D IIIs of *Flik* 41/J at 1030 hrs. In a textbook execution of Baracca's tactics for such an occasion, Parvis attacked while his leader flew off to the right and then closed from that quarter as Parvis completed his pass and veered off to strike at the enemy's left flank.

'The one engaged by Parvis, after a short fight, fled toward Latisana', Baracca reported. 'Mine, alarmed by my attack, continued to escape, going down in spirals. I fired short bursts until we arrived at 50 metres over the trees, myself always pursuing furiously from close behind, until the enemy stalled into the ground, smashing the aeroplane'.

Baracca's Hungarian opponent, Oblt Rudolf Szepessy-Sököll *Freiherr* von Négyes és Rénö, had scored his fourth and fifth victories over two Macchi L 3 flying boats just

OAW-built Albatros D IIIs and D Vs of *Jasta* 39 occupy Veldes aerodrome in October 1917 prior to the Austro-Hungarian counteroffensive at Caporetto. (Johann Visser via Jon Guttman)

ENGAGING THE ENEMY

By the time the SPAD VII and Albatros D III began encountering each other in early 1917, fighter pilots on both sides had a choice of gunsights. The earliest and simplest involved lining up a bead on a pylon with a ring about three inches in diameter, with four radial wires attached to an inner ring of 0.5- and 1-inch diameter, which allowed for the speed and direction of a moving target, as well as that of the pilot's own aeroplane.

A more sophisticated option was the Aldis, a tube that contained a series of lenses marked with two concentric rings, which transmitted parallel light rays. One advantage of this arrangement was that the centre was always directly on the axis of the sight, regardless of the position of the aimer's eye. Originally developed by the Aldis brothers in Sparkhill, Birmingham, in 1915, the 32-inch-long, 2-inch diameter collimated sight was a mainstay on British fighters.

The French developed the similar Le Crétien sight, which soon became a standard piece of equipment on all SPAD VIIs. Both tubes were hermetically sealed to contain an inert gas, which in turn prevented the lenses from fogging up in flight.

Albatros sights varied from ring and bead to simple tubular sights and, later in 1917, the Oigee gunsight, based on captured Aldis sights. The latter lacked the inert gas, resulting in fogged lenses that limited its usefulness.

In this scene, Capitano Francesco Baracca of *91ª Squadriglia*, flying a SPAD VII, closes in on Oeffag-built Albatros D III 153.54 of Austro-Hungarian *Flik* 41/J on 6 November 1917, the latter aircraft also trying to elude his wingman, Tenente Giuliano Parvis (at left). 'Firing occasionally, we get down to 50 metres over the trees', Baracca reported. 'I am always behind him until the enemy hit the ground, smashing the aeroplane. It was one of my best dogfights, the Austrian fighter pilot didn't get out of the aeroplane, so he must have been killed or badly hurt'. Crashing near Latisana at about 1000 hrs, Baracca's Hungarian opponent, five-victory ace Oblt Rudolf Szepessy-Sököll *Freiherr* von Négyes és Renö, was struck in the spine and died a short time later.

The pilot of Albatros D III (Oef) 253.75, assigned to the *Isonzoarmee* in July 1918, sports a parachute – a German conception which the Austro-Hungarians adopted late that summer, and frequently had occasion to use. Of some interest is the crudely applied thin, straight-sided cross on the fuselage, similar to the '*Balkenkreuz*' adopted by the Germans later that same year. (Greg VanWyngarden)

the day before. Hit in the spine, he managed to bring his D III (153.54) over the lines before crash-landing near Latisana. The ace died as he was being lifted from the cockpit.

Parvis' first opponent had escaped before he could fire a shot, and he rejoined Baracca in time to share in downing Szepessy-Sököll. However, the other Albatros (153.08) force-landed at Treviso, where its Slovenian pilot, Fw Iskra, told his Italian captors that he was defecting, along with unflattering remarks about professional jealousy among the Austrian flying officers.

On the 23rd Baracca and Tenente Gastone Novelli were jointly credited with an Albatros D III. 'I took off on patrol with Maj Baracca at 1505 hrs', Novelli reported. 'An enemy fighter was spotted over Montello, and it was attacked by the patrol leader at a height of about 3,500m (11,400ft). The pilot defended himself, manoeuvring and trying to reach his lines. I entered the fight, firing about 60 rounds. The enemy aircraft crashed into the River Piave, coming to rest upside down on the river bed'. The German pilot, Vzfw Karl Überschär of *Jasta* 39, was killed.

By 10 November the Italians had taken up new defensive positions south of the Piave and the front stabilised. SPAD XIIIs began arriving in *91ª Squadriglia* later that month, although Baracca was not impressed with them. 'It doesn't matter if the VII is equipped with a single gun', he wrote. 'Provided you are a good fighter, a single gun is just enough'.

Although *77ª* and *91ª Squadriglie* pilots did well in SPAD VIIs, most *squadriglie* were equipped with the Hanriot HD 1, and *91ª* was entirely equipped with the SPAD XIII by 15 June 1918 when the Austro-Hungarian army made its last breakthrough attempt at the Piave. At *77ª*, however, Tenente Lombardi was still flying a SPAD VII that day when he claimed an D III, which he described as being red with white crosses and a black hand insignia, south of Biagio. On the 16th he downed D III 153.222, flown by Ltn d R Hans Wolfschütz of *Flik* 41/J, bringing his total to eight.

STATISTICS AND ANALYSIS

The principal battles in which the SPAD VII and the Albatros D III served as the cutting edges of their respective air arms were the Allied offensives at Arras and the Aisne in the spring of 1917 and the Battle of Caporetto and its aftermath in October-November 1917. Serious analysis of their performance in both areas comes with its own caveats, some of which apply to any other fighter types during World War I.

By the end of January 1917 the SPAD VII had proven its worth, but the Albatros D III had exhibited a disturbing structural weakness of the wing cellule that necessitated its withdrawal from the front for reinforcement of the lower plane. Over the next two months the earlier Albatros D II and Halberstadt fighters had a 'last hurrah'. The D III's wing modifications were satisfactorily completed in time for 'Bloody April', but even then its phased-in return to frontline service meant that many Albatrosen encountered by both the French and the British could be older, but proven, D IIs or even D Is.

The French units, too, were in a state of transition, based on production delays that kept Nieuport sesquiplanes on full strength in some squadrons and on partial strength even in units that had been slated for complete re-equipment. This in turn meant that many SPAD-equipped

A SPAD VII of SPA78 brought down in German lines typifies the fate of scores of Allied fighters that were often captured fully intact, thus providing confirmation for the Albatros pilots who claimed them. (Greg VanWyngarden)

escadrilles officially kept their 'N' rather than 'SPA' designators for months pending the completion of the phased transition process. Under the circumstances, there would be many cases of German pilots mixing up the two types in their combat reports.

Though not prone to do so as often as the British, both the French and Germans were quite capable of mistaking a foe diving away for one taking its final plunge. On 31 May 1917, for example, Capt Kiyotake Shigeno of N26 was leading Sous-Lt André Dezarrois and MdL Auguste Pouchelle on a patrol when they were attacked by three 'monoplaces'. Pouchelle, wounded and hard-pressed, dived to earth and force-landed in French lines. The only German SPAD claim that day was by Ltn Josef Veltjens of *Jasta* 14, who was credited with his fourth victory over Oulches. However, Pouchelle, who had already survived being driven down in French lines in flames on 10 July 1916, and being wounded on 18 August, survived this misfortune as well. He went on to fly with N26 and later SPA67 to the end of the war.

Albatros D III pilots claimed 17 French and ten British SPADs in April 1917. French SPAD VII losses in that time came to 11 men missing or captured, along with one pilot known to have come down in Allied lines wounded, while the RFC lost seven SPAD pilots and one wounded. The three German Albatros pilots killed were all victims of French SPADs, in addition to which Oblt Rudolf Berthold of *Jasta* 14 was wounded by a French antagonist on 24 April. The 11 British claims of Albatrosen shot down that month, ten of which were 'out of control', do not stand up to scrutiny that well, although they may have included some machines forced to land, just as some of their own and some French cases occasionally went 'confirmed' to their German counterparts.

Checking claims against losses during the Second Battle of the Aisne suggests that the French were marginally less precise than the Germans in appraising a victory against eyewitness accounts and actual enemy losses. It is also apparent that the French, whichever fighters they flew, were taking somewhat the worst of it against the Albatros. That unpleasant fact was driven home especially hard in the sudden spate of casualties

BELOW LEFT
MdL Auguste Pouchelle of N26 was credited to Ltn Josef Veltjens of *Jasta* 14 on 31 May 1917, but he came down in French lines wounded and lived to fly and fight again through to the end of the war. (SHAA B88.4471)

BELOW RIGHT
Lt Albert Deullin of N3, shown with the squadron mascot 'Parasol', at first believed in as small as two-man flights being best for challenging the enemy, but after the death of his friend René Dorme he wrote that larger, massed formations would be necessary to match the German *Jastas*. (Louis Risacher Collection via Jon Guttman)

suffered in the elite 'Stork' *escadrilles* of GC12 in May 1917, including the serious wounding of Alfred Heurtaux on the 5th and the death of René Dorme on the 25th.

The RFC began 'Bloody April' with No. 19 Sqn as its only fully equipped SPAD unit, with No. 23 Sqn completing its transition to the French scouts. Their strength pales against the four Nieuport 17 squadrons also listed in the British order of battle, along with three Sopwith Pup squadrons, one with new Bristol F 2A Fighters, one with new SE 5s, two still using obsolescent DH 2s and two with FE 8s, as well as two RNAS Sopwith Triplane squadrons.

Encounters between Albatrosen and RFC SPADs during the spring of 1917 were thus incidental to the greater number involving other British types, all of which did their proportionate share of suffering at the hands of the *Jastas*. Equally proportionate is the amount of overclaiming and counting of 'out of control' victories among all British fighter units, which enhanced pilots' scores but gave an inaccurate impression of the attrition actually being inflicted on the enemy.

Checking claims against actual losses in Italy proves to be inherently more difficult than over the Western Front, starting with the factor of aircraft recognition, which was dismal on both sides. Italian reference to an 'Albatros' almost invariably meant a two-seater, particularly the Brandenburg C I. Enemy fighters were seldom mentioned by name, and most of the time the Italians – and the British, for that matter – tended to confuse Albatros with Phönix and Aviatik types.

The Austro-Hungarians were no better, incessantly mistaking Nieuports for SPADs and vice versa. Much to the Italians' chagrin, they also had a penchant for assuming any radial-engine biplane scout they encountered in 1918 to be a British-flown 'Sopwith Camel', even when it was an Italian Hanriot HD 1.

The erratic nature of witness' perceptions of damage inflicted on an opponent, endemic to all sides, was exacerbated in Italy by the alpine terrain over which they fought. Nevertheless, a comparison favours the relative strictness of Italian confirmation standards over that of their Habsburg counterparts. Examples of slipshod Austro-Hungarian confirmations are evident in some of the earliest clashes. On 18 August 1917, *Flik* 24's Ltn d R Josef Friedrich was escorting two Brandenburg C Is of his unit when one was attacked over Monte Lisser by what he identified as a SPAD. After a furious combat, the SPAD apparently crashed in enemy territory at Grigno, after which the Brandenburg's observer took a photograph of Friedrich coming up alongside his aeroplane, his left fist raised in jubilant triumph.

The closest Italian match to the incident comes from the log of *79ª Squadriglia*, in which Sergente Antonio Reale attacked a two-seater, got into a sharp combat with its escort and finally broke off the action with his

Rejoining the Brandenburg C I two-seater he was escorting in Albatros D III (Oef) 53.38, Ltn d R Josef Friedrich of *Flik* 24 raises his fist in triumph after shooting down a 'SPAD' on 18 August 1917. In fact, his opponent, Sergente Antonio Reale of *79ª Squadriglia*, made it safely home to Istrana aerodrome in his damaged Nieuport 17! (Greg VanWyngarden)

aeroplane (a Nieuport 17, not a SPAD VII) damaged, but not badly enough to prevent his returning to his aerodrome at Istrana.

Italy's leading ace, Francesco Baracca, had numerous run-ins with Albatros aces, killing one and being claimed by at least three. On 15 September he fought with an Austro-Hungarian fighter until his gun jammed, at which point he disengaged, no doubt by the best means for a SPAD – diving away. His adversary was apparently Zugsführer Julius Arigi of *Flik* 55/J, flying Albatros D III (Oef) 115.15, whose claim over a SPAD 'forced to land' was confirmed by *Feldartilleriebrigade* Nr 16 for his 13th victory. Notwithstanding that, Baracca returned to Santa Caterina aerodrome unharmed.

Eight days later, on the 23rd, Baracca took on four enemy fighters over Lovke, but failed to down his first target and found himself under attack from the others. Baracca extricated himself easily, probably in a power dive that might have emitted enough excess smoke for the Austrians, including infantry witnesses, to confirm a SPAD VII with French cockades downed near Novi Vas in flames. This was jointly credited to Oblt d R Ernst Strohschneider and Zugsführer Nandor Udvardy of *Flik* 42/J, the third victory for each.

For comparison, Baracca's and other Italians' successes in the SPAD VII can often be traced to an enemy loss, such as the Albatros D III credited to him and Parvis on 6 November 1917, killing Oblt Rudolf Szepessy-Sököll *Freiherr* von Negyes és Renö of *Flik* 41/J. He and Tenente Novelli also enjoyed success on the 23rd, their claim corresponding to the death of Fw Karl Überschär of *Jasta* 39. Finally, Baracca was also flying a SPAD VII on 22 May 1918 when he and Sergente Mario D'Urso destroyed Albatros D III (Oef) 153.155 near Cimidolmo, killing Fähnrich Ernst Pontalti of *Flik* 51/J.

Not all Italian claims hold up as well. On 10 August 1918 Tenente Sebastiano Bedendo and Sergente Augusto Levrero of *71ª Squadriglia* were escorting a Pomilio

Eight-victory ace Sottotenente Ernesto Cabruna flew SPAD VII S1420, decorated with the coat of arms of his hometown of Tortona, with *79ª Squadriglia* to the end of the war. The restored aeroplane can be seen in the Italian Air Force Museum at Vigna di Valle near Rome. (*Roberto Gentilli*)

COMANDANTE
ERNESTO CABRUNA
DA TORTONA
MEDAGLIA D'ORO AL V. M.
GUERRA MONDIALE 1915-1918
MEDAGLIA D'ORO AL VALORE FIUMANO

SP 3 over Monte Pasubio when they spotted five enemy fighters. They promptly engaged them and claimed to have destroyed one with a black and white chequerboard on the fuselage. Bedendo returned with holes in the upper wing and struts of his SPAD VII. The Austro-Hungarian record has *Flik* 3/J engaging an 'SVA 5' escorted by two fighters, of which one of the latter was sent down to a somersaulting crash-landing at Monte Pasubio and was credited as the seventh victory for the unit CO, Oblt Friedrich Navratil, flying Albatros D III (Oef) 253.06. Although the Italian SPAD pilots were jointly credited with the enemy fighter they had claimed, *Flik* 3/J suffered no casualties that day either.

Two general conclusions might be drawn from the two fighters' encounters. One is that the SPAD VII's single machine gun, Baracca's comments notwithstanding, was a recurring handicap to pilots whose marksmanship fell short of his own when facing the twin guns of an Albatros, and its chronic tendency to jam put many an Allied pilot in jeopardy – including Baracca himself, as recounted earlier. On the other hand, in spite of the inherent weaknesses of the Albatros D III's sesquiplane wing structure, the measures taken to reinforce it, combined with its pilots' knowledge of the fighter's limitations and their well-practised tactics to make the most of it and their generally defensive role, kept them at least a match for the SPAD in the crucible of combat.

Leading SPAD VII Albatros D III Killers

Aéronautique Militaire			
Pilot	Escadrille	D IIIs	Total
Lucien Jailler	N15	3	12
Armand Pinsard	N78	3	27
Pierre de Cazenove de Pradines	N81	1	7
Jean Chaput	N57	1	16
René Dorme	N3	1	23
Jean Dubois de Gennes	N57	1	5
Gabriel Guérin	N15	1	23
Marcel Hauss	N57	1	5
Marcel Henriot	N65	1	5
Gilbert de Guingand	N48	1	8
René Fonck	N103	1	75
Alexandre Marty	N77	1	5
Marcel Nogues	N57	1	13
Edmond Pillon	N82	1	8

RFC			
Pilot	**Squadron**	**D IIIs**	**Total**
William J. C. Kennedy-Cochran-Patrick	23	11	21
Douglas U. McGregor	23	8	12
Conn Standish O'Grady	23	5	9
Thomas A. Doran	23	4	7
Oliver C. Bryson	19	3	12
Frederick Sowrey	19	3	12
Clive W. Warman	23	3	12
Robert M. Farquhar	23	2	6

Aviazione del Regio Ecercito			
Pilot	***Squadriglie***	**D IIIs**	**Total**
Gastone Novelli	*91ª*	3	7
Pier Ruggiero Piccio	*91ª*	3	24
Flaminio Avet	*70ª*	2	8
Francesco Baracca	*91ª*	2	34
Francesco Carlo Lombardi	*77ª*	2	7
Ferruccio Ranza	*91ª*	2	17
Giovanni Ancillotto	*77ª*	1	11
Sebastiani Bedendo	*71ª*	1	7
Cesare Magistrini	*91ª*	1	6
Giuliano Parvis	*91ª*	1	6

Leading Albatros D III SPAD VII Killers

Luftstreitskräfte			
Pilot	***Jasta(s)***	**SPAD VIIs**	**Total**
Heinrich Claudius Kroll	9	5	33
Josef Veltjens	14	4	35
Rudolf Berthold	14 & 18	3	44
Oskar *Frhr* von Boenigk	21	3	26
Heinrich Gontermann	15	3	39
Hartmut Baldamus	9	2	18
Hans Bowski	14	2	5

Paul Henning A. T. von Osterroht	12	2	7
Lothar *Frhr* von Richthofen	11	2	40
Kurt Wolff	11	2	33
Paul Aue	10	1	10
Hans Bethge	30	1	20
Paul Billik	12	1	31
Heinrich Bongartz	36	1	33
Franz Brandt	19	1	10
Julius Buckler	17	1	36
Hermann Frommherz	'Boelcke'	1	32
Wolfgang Güttler	24	1	8
Alfred Hübner	36	1	6
Reinhold Jörke	12	1	14
Otto Kissenberth	16	1	20
Wilhelm Leusch	19	1	5
Bruno Loerzer	26	1	44
Hermann Pfeiffer	9	1	11
Manfred *Frhr* von Richthofen	11	1	80
Karl Fritz Schattauer	23	1	9
Otto Schmidt	32	1	20
Kurt Schneider	5	1	15
Edgar Scholtz	Kest 10	1	6
Adolf *Ritter* von Tutschek	12	1	27
Ernst Udet	15	1	62
Richard Wenzl	31	1	12

KuK Luftfahrtruppen			
Pilot	**Flik**	**SPAD VIIs**	**Total**
Ernst Strohschneider	42/J	2	15
Nandor Udvardy	42/J	2	8
Benno Fiala *Ritter* von Fernbrugg	51/J	1	28
Josef Friedrich	24	1	7
Friedrich Navratil	3/J	1	10
Karl Nikitsch	39	1	6
Franz Rudorfer	51/J	1	11

AFTERMATH

'Bloody April' marked a zenith in Albatros' fortunes that continued into May and June 1917, even while its new 'lightened' D V began replacing the D III in the *Jagdstaffeln*. Disillusionment followed in July, however, as reports of buffeting and failures of the D V's lower wing, together with the discovery that its performance was not that much improved, made many German pilots nostalgic for their older D IIIs.

The *Amerika Programm's* requirement for uninterrupted fighter production gave the discredited sesquiplanes a reprieve. Albatros beefed up the D V and in August introduced the reinforced D Va. *Idflieg* ordered an eventual 1,600 D Vas, but interestingly hedged its bets in September by giving Albatros' Scheidemühl subsidiary, OAW a last order for D IIIs modified with D V rudders.

Ltn Franz Ray, CO of *Jasta* 49, poses in an OAW-built Albatros D III in the summer of 1918. Pending the belated delivery of Fokker D VIIs, *Jasta* 49 was apparently equipped with OAW-built D IIIs as late as July 1918 due to Ray's preference for these proven fighters over newer types. (Heinz Nowarra album via Jon Guttman)

Other fighter candidates appeared in the late summer of 1917, yet German pilots generally favoured the Albatros, with all of its faults, over the robust but sluggish Pfalz D III. The Fokker Dr I triplane, with its innovative wooden box cantilever structure, displayed spectacular climb and manoeuvrability, but wing and aileron failures due to poor quality control delayed deliveries in significant numbers until January 1918.

Thus, like it or not, the Germans spent the balance of 1917 making do with Albatros sesquiplanes. The tactics they had honed earlier that year, expanded by the grouping of *Jastas* within local *Jagdgruppen* or roving *Jagdgeschwader*, helped them hold their own against a variety of improved Allied fighters until the superb Fokker D VII biplane made its debut in the spring of 1918.

Even then, the old but proven D III soldered on in some *Amerika Programm* or home defence units well into 1918 until enough Fokker D VIIs were available to replace them. At the end of April that year, the German fighter force included 174 Albatros D IIIs, along with 928 D Vas and 131 D Vs, 433 Pfalz D IIIas, 171 Fokker Dr Is and 19 Fokker D VIIs. There were still 52 D IIIs listed as operational in the *Luftstreitskräfte's* last fighter inventory on 31 August 1918, compared to 307 D Vas and 20 D Vs.

On the Italian front, Oeffag's superior workmanship – albeit at the cost of speed and quantity of production – gave the Albatros D III a new lease on life, made all the livelier with more powerful engines than its German counterparts ever dreamt of using. By 1918 it was indisputably Austria-Hungary's best fighter, but doomed to be overwhelmed by Italy's armadas of SPADs, Nieuports and Hanriots.

As resurgent structural problems with the Albatros D V kept the D III useful long past its shelf life, so chronic reduction gear failures in the SPAD XIII's Hispano-Suiza 8b engine kept the SPAD VII, with its more reliable 8Ab, a mainstay in French *escadrilles*, as well as the Italian *77ª* and *91ª Squadriglie* and the American 103rd and 139th Aero Squadrons, well into the summer of 1918. Even at the time of the armistice, many SPAD XIII-equipped *escadrilles* kept a backup complement of VIIs,

Production delays resulted in SPAD VIIs still trickling into Nieuport-equipped *escadrilles* in the quieter sectors well into 1918. For example, earlier that year N87's Nieuport 24s and 27s were complemented by SPAD S1562 '1', flown by the CO, Capt Pierre Azire, and by S1765 '2'. The latter machine, normally assigned to Sous-Lt Jean Dehesdin, was being flown by LFC member Cpl Thomas Hitchcock Jr on 6 March when he was shot down by Ltn Georg Weiner of *Kampfeinsitzer Staffel* 3 and captured. (SHAA B96.4155)

This newly delivered SPAD VII bears the tiger's head marking of SPA162, which gave up the last of its Nieuports in May 1918. (Jon Guttman)

and a few newly formed American units were equipped with VIIs until more XIIIs became available.

While many British pilots liked the SPAD VII, SPAD XIIIs replaced them in No. 23 Sqn at the end of 1917. Between February and March 1918, however, both Nos. 19 and 23 Sqns were re-equipped with an indigenously built Hispano-Suiza-powered fighter, the Sopwith 5F1 Dolphin, which proved to be outstanding in its own right.

Although their moments of supremacy were short-lived, the SPAD VII and the Albatros D III remained ubiquitous workhorses throughout World War I, and continued to serve in a variety of air arms into the 1920s. In fact, the SPAD VII and Albatros D III (Oef) served side by side in the air force of a resurrected Poland as it fought Russian Bolshevik invaders in 1920.

SPAD VII S11420 was assigned to 1Lt Clifford E. Andrews of the 138th Aero Squadron, 5th Pursuit Group. Narrowly missing the war, the group was formed four days after the armistice and served with the Allied occupation forces based at Coblenz in 1919. (Jon Guttman)

FURTHER READING

BOOKS

Chassard, Marc, *René Dorme et Joseph Guiguet, La Guerre aérienne de deux as* (Éditions aux Arts, Lyon, 2002)

Franks, Norman, Guest, Russell and Bailey, Frank W., *Bloody April … Black September* (Grub Street, London, 1995)

Franks, Norman, Bailey, Frank and Duiven, Ric, *The Jasta War Chronology* (Grub Street, London, 1998)

Gordon, Dennis, *Lafayette Escadrille Pilot Biographies* (The Doughboy Historical Society, Missoula, MT, 1991, p. 244)

Grosz, Peter M., *Albatros D III* (Albatros Publications Ltd, Berkhamsted, Herts, 2003)

Kilduff, Peter, *Richthofen – Beyond the Legend of the Red Baron* (Arms & Armour Press, London, 1993)

Kilduff, Peter, *"That's My Bloody Plane", The World War I Experiences of Major Cecil Montgomery-Moore DFC, as told to Peter Kilduff* (The Prequot Press, Chester, Conn, 1975)

Kowalski, Tomasz J., *SPAD S A1-S VII.C1* (OW Kagero, Lublin, Poland)

Merrill, G. K., *Jagdstaffel 5, Vol. 1* (Albatros Productions Ltd, Berkhamsted, Herts, 2004)

Revell, Alex, *British Single-Seater Fighter Squadrons on the Western Front in World War I* (Schiffer Publishing Ltd, Atglen, PA, 2006)

Shores, Christopher, Franks, Norman and Guest, Russell, *Above the Trenches* (Grub Street, London, 1990)

Tesar, Mgr Petr Aharon, *Albatros D II & D III Oeffag* (JaPo, Hradec Králové, Czech Republic, 1998)

MAGAZINES

de Cazenove de Pradines, Pierre, 'Triumphs and Tribulations', *Cross & Cockade (USA) Journal*, Vol. 21, No. 1, Spring 1980, p. 72

Grosz, Peter M., 'The Agile & Aggressive Albatros', *Air Enthusiast Quarterly*, No. 1, pp. 36–51

Lombardi, Francis, 'Gli Amici di Marcon 1918-1978', *Cross & Cockade Great Britain Journal*, Vol. 12, No. 3, Autumn 1981, pp. 118–30

INDEX